Better Homes and Gardens®

COME HOME
TO
COUNTRY

BETTER HOMES AND GARDENS® BOOKS
Editor: Gerald M. Knox
Art Director: Ernest Shelton
Managing Editor: David A. Kirchner
Editorial Project Managers: Liz Anderson, James D. Blume,
    Marsha Jahns, Rosanne Weber Mattson

Senior Furnishings Editor, Books: Gayle Goodson Butler

Associate Art Directors: Neoma Thomas, Linda Ford Vermie,
    Randall Yontz
Assistant Art Directors: Lynda Haupert, Harijs Priekulis, Tom Wegner
Graphic Designers: Mary Schlueter Bendgen, Mike Burns, Brian Wignall
Art Production: Director, John Berg; Associate, Joe Heuer; Office Manager,
    Michaela Lester

President, Book Group: Jeramy Lanigan
Vice President, Retail Marketing: Jamie L. Martin
Vice President, Administrative Services: Rick Rundall

BETTER HOMES AND GARDENS® MAGAZINE
President, Magazine Group: James A. Autry
Editorial Director: Doris Eby
Editorial Services Director: Duane L. Gregg
Furnishings and Design Editor: Shirley Van Zante

MEREDITH CORPORATION OFFICERS
Chairman of the Executive Committee: E. T. Meredith III
Chairman of the Board: Robert A. Burnett
President: Jack D. Rehm

COME HOME TO COUNTRY
Editor: Gayle Goodson Butler
Editorial Project Manager: Marsha Jahns
Graphic Designer: Tom Wegner
Electronic Text Processor: Paula Forest
Contributing Writers: Denise L. Caringer, Jane Austin McKeon,
    Sharon Novotne O'Keefe, Rosemary Rennicke, Pamela J. Wilson

There's something about country that calls us home. Maybe it's the comfort of honest, easy furnishings, or the character of the handmade. Or perhaps it's a yearning for a life-style that's simpler and softer around the edges. Whatever the allure, Americans—from city to heartland—are responding, making country one of the nation's most enduring and inventive decorating styles. Better Homes and Gardens® *Come Home to Country* captures country as it is today: fresh, yet timeless; beautiful, yet unpretentious; and, always, comfortable to the core.

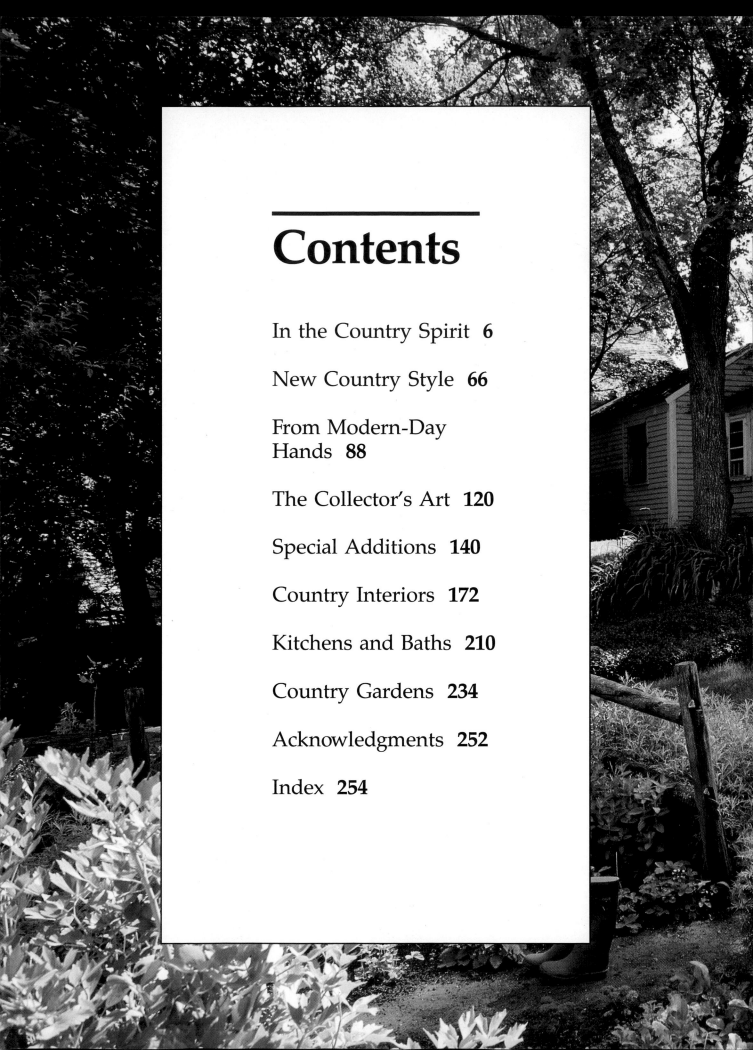

Contents

In the Country Spirit

No matter where you live, if your home celebrates heritage, hospitality, and simple pleasures, you've come home to country. Welcome to six homes that share the country spirit.

Back to Home Base

It's not every family that buys a house sight unseen. But special circumstances led Steve and Linda Benson to do just that. The couple and their two school-age daughters were living in Europe when they learned that the 1850s Massachusetts farmhouse at *left* was on the market. Knowing that they'd be returning to their native New England in four years' time, they decided to buy the suburban Boston dwelling, then rent it out until their return.

When the Bensons came home to America in 1983, the Georgian-style house stood ready, waiting, and in dire need of redoing. Everything—wiring, plumbing, ceilings, walls, and floors—called for repair or restoration, but the Bensons were not put off. Indeed, they had anticipated a rehab project, and happily got busy with the task at hand.

Once the nitty-gritty work was out of the way, the Bensons turned their attention to decorating. During the last few years of living abroad, the couple spent hours shopping for furnishings and accessories for their new home, and now—at last—they could unpack their finds and put them in place.

continued

9

Except for some judicious re-modeling in the kitchen and master bathroom, the Bensons left the interior of the farm-house basically intact. The living room—actually two back-to-back parlors—posed the biggest challenge for Linda, an interior designer. Should the two parlors be treated as one big room or as separate, yet decoratively cohesive, spaces? Linda opted for the latter solution, turning the back parlor, *opposite*, into a family room, and the front parlor (a glimpse of which can be seen *above*) into a cozy conversation area.

The back parlor, with its down-filled sofa and easy chair, focuses on an antique Danish armoire, which has been outfitted as an entertainment center. The coffee table—a cut-down antique kitchen table—hails from England. Ditto the child's antique chair and the Victorian chair that flank the table.

continued

Back to
Home Base
(continued)

Back to
Home Base
(continued)

If there's one thing Linda Benson can't stand, it's clutter. She avoids excess by paring down, by mixing country antiques and accessories with clean-lined contemporary pieces, and by knowing when to stop.

The front parlor, *opposite*, beautifully expresses her philosophy of restraint. Here, casual seating pieces combine with carefully selected wooden antiques and just a smattering of accessories. The modular sofa and wicker chair are covered in a warm white cotton—a good background for the pillows in a mix of flowered chintz, solid polished cotton, and woven jacquards. A small antique English trunk serves as a coffee table—

and as a reminder to the Bensons of their years spent abroad.

What ties this room to the nearby back parlor is the color scheme. In both spaces, walls are painted white, and woodwork is painted buff. Identical, too, are the window treatments: floor-length muslin curtains edged in a cranberry-colored, polished cotton trim.

Like the parlor, the sunny dining room, *above*, is a clutter-free blend of old and new. The pine table and wicker chairs are reproductions of classics; the glass-fronted cupboard and the Welsh dresser, just barely seen in the foreground, are companionable antiques.

continued

In remodeling the farmhouse kitchen/keeping room, the Bensons incorporated an old shed into the room, enlarging the space considerably. Before remodeling, the antiquated kitchen ended where the island, *above*, now stands, and the space was cramped and dreary. The former shed is now a fully equipped kitchen, with a generous skylight and tall casement windows to provide a lovely garden view.

To retain a quality of age, the Bensons incorporated a few elements of the shed into their kitchen design: The structural beams, the old red door, and the small windows that flank it are all originals. The Mexican terra cotta tile floor is new, but has been waxed to a mellow finish so it will blend with the pumpkin pine floorboards in the adjoining room.

What used to be the kitchen area is now a charming keeping room, *opposite*, complete with the original 1850s fireplace. The oiled teak table and chairs are the kind often seen in Irish pubs. Indeed, these pieces were made by Al O'Dea of Taum, Ireland, and thus are the real McCoys. The Oriental runner that graces the table is said to have once graced a camel's back. Illuminating this atmospheric setting is a new version of an old-style chandelier.

continued

There *are* risks in buying a house sight unseen, or better said, in buying furniture for a house one has never set foot in. The Bensons, for example, were under the mistaken impression that their New England farmhouse contained a large master bedroom—large enough for the pine four-poster they bought in Germany. But not so. The bed was so big and the room so small that the posts had to be cut down and the bed—in order to fit at all—had to be placed at an angle. But never mind. As far as the Bensons are concerned, the presence of a fireplace more than makes up for the room's tight squeeze.

Willing as they were to put up with a closet-size master bedroom, the Bensons could not tolerate bumping elbows in their minuscule, outdated bathroom. To improve matters, they commandeered a small bedroom and merged it with the existing bath to create the spacious combination bath/dressing room, *above.* With its white laminate double-sink vanity, his-and-her closets, blush pink walls, and wide-plank floors, the bath is a magical melding of old and new. Small touches—a hat rack for towels, an old corner chair, and a catchall pine table—add to the room's one-of-a-kind appeal.

Styled in Stone

It was just over a year ago that Tom and Ruth Tempel Touhill purchased Stoneledge Farm, *left,* a 200-acre habitat complete with a 19th-century stone house, a barn, a guesthouse, and a greenhouse. The couple's original intent was to spend the workweek at their home in St. Louis, then escape to Stoneledge on weekends. But something happened. Ruth, a successful interior designer, found herself spending more and more time at the farm, fixing up the old stone house and turning the barn into an antiques shop. Tom, an advertising executive and outdoor enthusiast, developed an interest in returning the land to working-farm status.

Finding that weekends in the country are just not enough, the Touhills now plan to sell their city dwelling and maintain only a small *pied à terre* there. Their primary residence will be Stoneledge, so named because a solid ribbon of stone ledges surrounds the farm. Thus far, the Touhills know little of the farm's history, but they do know that the land was once inhabited by American Indians and was later deeded by the U.S. government to Daniel Boone and family.

continued

19

Some people, Ruth Touhill among them, have a wonderful ability for piecing disparate elements into an aesthetically pleasing whole. The interior of Stoneledge, with its tantalizing assemblage of oddments and antiques, bespeaks Ruth's enviable talent.

Furnishings in the stone-walled sun-room, *left*, include a wicker sofa that Ruth purchased 25 years ago, a wicker writing table with a rustic wood top, and a colorful hooked rug found at a garage sale. The coffee table is an old at-home school desk that Ruth purchased from a neighbor when she was a teenager and, says Ruth, "I've been schlepping it around ever since."

More of Ruth's mixing techniques can be seen in the close-up, *above*. Here, a contemporary glass flower vase is teamed with a majolica pitcher and fruit-filled plates, an Indian basket tray lined with lace, an old English leather letter holder, and assorted books.   *continued*

21

Styled in Stone

(continued)

R uth's tastes run the gamut, from American country, to art deco, to art nouveau, to anything and everything English. So ardent an Anglophile is Ruth that several times a year she travels to Great Britain to buy antiques. What she doesn't claim for her own use she sells to her clients or displays in her barn-turned-shop.

Interestingly, although the Touhills' living room, *right*, calls to mind a cottage in Cornwall, there's only one English item—a small tilt-top table—in the room. Everything else is American, and, what's more, most of the furnishings were fortuitous finds. The easy chairs, purchased at a junk shop for $15 each, "were one of my best buys," says Ruth, an inveterate bargain hunter. Covered in a floral chintz fabric, the chairs set the tone for elegant country charm.

The deep rose brocade that covers the sleep sofa was yet another bargain: Prior to buying Stoneledge, Ruth purchased 30 yards of the fabric at a discount fabric store—not knowing what she'd do with it, but unable to resist its beauty and its tempting price tag.

Also artful—and inexpensive—is the coffee table. It's made from four balcony-style balustrades and topped with a slab of glass. *continued*

22

Perhaps because it contains an English rocking horse and assorted lord-of-the-manor outdoor gear, Tom Touhill refers to the dining room/den as "the fox and hound room." Originally a kitchen, complete with a dirt floor, this room today is a favorite spot for the Touhills and their friends.

A large English pine trestle table, *right*, surrounded by circa-1810 stools, is perfect for informal entertaining. At the far end of the table is a fine 18th-century English settle with a horsehair seat and a piece of old hand-loomed carpet casually draped over the back. The framed art that adorns the stone wall are landscape etchings that Ruth had been saving for 20 years. Placed on a ledge beneath the etchings are several pieces of old hotel silver from the Albert Pick Hotel in Chicago.

The sitting area, *above*, is furnished with a pair of faithful old sofas, recently re-covered (for the fourth time!) in a simple forest green fabric. A pine trunk serves as a coffee table and a display surface.

Accessories—English walking sticks, umbrellas, hats, and other country life accoutrements—are as serviceable as they are whimsical.

Down by The Seaside

For city dwellers Eileen and Jack Connors, country awaits in Cape Cod. Specifically, it awaits at their seaside retreat, a place where they and their four children seek peace and pleasure during the warm-weather months.

Surrounded by sand dunes, sea breezes, and salty air, the 1940s cottage has been completely refurbished to meet the Connorses' needs. Marjorie Penny, a talented interior de-signer, took charge of the rehab, inside and out. Small rooms were melded into a casual, open plan, and windows were added to capture ocean views.

Decoratively, too, the cottage is pure delight, with settings that draw on, yet update, country themes. Colors are as fresh a fine summer day, textures are as natural as the wicker *above,* and the countrified furnishings are perfectly suited for a relaxed way of life. *continued*

Down by
The Seaside
(continued)

Paneled walls painted white
and pickled hardwood floors
set the stage for the Connorses'
casual summer-house scheme.
The living area, *above* and *right,*
features a gathering of cushy,
down-filled seating pieces, some
covered in coordinated prints,
others in solid periwinkle blue.
The color scheme mimics the
hues from the harbor, as seen
from the windows, *above*.

An antique Dutch cupboard
vies with the view as the room's
major see-worthy attraction.
The handsome piece, with its
unusual, three-sided bonnet,
was restored by John Anderson
of Boston, a custom decorative
painter. High-skirted chairs
flanking the cupboard are covered in a fanciful print fabric
depicting snails at the seashore.
continued

The Connorses love the informality of country furnishings, and after a day at the beach, the clan loves to gather in the casual dining room/ kitchen, *right* and *above*. An antique English table welcomes all comers, as do the new bentwood-style rattan chairs, painted blueberry and upholstered in sturdy white leather. Everything is relaxed here, from the nubby rag rug to the backless wicker lounge that separates the kitchen from the dining area.

Even the room itself promises respite: The new fieldstone fireplace is a warming presence on cool, cloudy days, and the painted cathedral ceiling provides blue skies regardless of inclement weather. Adding colorful charm to the fireplace mantel is a parade of potted begonias and—befitting the oceanside location—a silk screen of sunglasses executed by a local artist.

The all-white kitchen, though contemporary, is accessorized with baskets, jugs, and other country collectibles.

continued

The master bedroom is a
place to retire, not just at
night, but whenever the Connorses seek solitude. Located
just off the foyer, the room carries out design themes used
throughout the house. Wall-to-
wall carpet repeats the blue-
and-white lattice motif of the
living room rugs; the paneled
walls, again, are painted sea-
foam white. Furnishings, including a caned four-poster, a
plump sofa, and an armless
chair, invite the Connorses to
get comfortable; wicker and an
antique pine armoire add mellow accents. The cozy desk area,
above, is for homework.

In the Country Spirit
Irish
Inspiration

Filled as it is with wonderful American country antiques, Mary and Pat Gilroy's English Tudor house owes its allure to Ireland, or—better said—to Mary's Irish-immigrant mother. When Mary was a child, her mother would speak longingly and lovingly of the old country, describing in detail the comforting folksiness of her girlhood home, and creating for Mary a nostalgic yearning for a place she had never seen.

For years, Mary carried this image of home in her head and her heart. Then, as Irish luck would have it, she met antiques dealer Gene Reed. Not only has Gene helped Mary create the home of her dreams, but she's shown her how to do it using all American antiques.

continued

34

Although there's not a single Irish antique in the Gilroys' house, the ambience is old-country warm and inviting. Every room is filled with folksy acquisitions, the kind that Mary's mother no doubt would have loved.

Collectibles of all kinds are apt to tempt Mary, and she's not put off by antiques that have been "reworked" or are imperfect—especially if they're priced right. This nonpurist approach not only has benefited the Gilroys' bank account, but also has enabled Mary to amass sizable collections in a relatively short (nine-year) period.

In addition to being an impatient collector, Mary can be impetuous, too. "I fall in love with pieces and buy them whether I have a place for them or not," she admits. And it's true. The baskets, stoneware, shop signs, and decoys that grace the den, *left* and *above,* are but a sampling of the examples Mary owns. Where's the overflow? In storage, ready to emerge when the Gilroys move to a larger house.

continued

Enamored as she is with
American country antiques,
Mary doesn't shun good reproductions or contemporary
pieces. Examples of all can be
found throughout the house.
What the Gilroys seek are furnishings that can be used on an
everyday basis, not just admired
from afar. Indeed, Mary won't
buy an antique unless it's easy
to live with, and she doesn't
mind an occasional nick or
scratch. Gene Reed aptly describes the Gilroys' possessions
as "usable works of art."

Mary's decorative, yet practical, approach begins in the en-
tryway, *above.* Sturdy ladder-
back chairs stand at attention
on each side of a lovely grain-
painted blanket chest, still used
as intended, for storage. Even
the old checkerboards, placed in
an artistic stair-step arrangement, are always ready for a
game. The horse, though once
functional, is now off its rocker.

The dining room, too, combines aesthetic appeal with utilitarian function. Taking center
stage, *right,* is a well-worn harvest table, a quilt-bedecked
wing chair, and a quintet of
humble hand-painted chairs.
The chandelier, like all ceiling
fixtures in the house, is fitted
with real candles.

continued

Not one to be ruled by floor plans or convention, Mary has arranged the living room, *left* and *above*, to suit her definition of comfort. In an interesting role reversal, she placed a mustard-colored table and chairs in front of the fireplace, and relegated the sofa and other seating pieces to the room's perimeters. The offbeat arrangement works well for Mary and Pat's life-style, and—not surprisingly—it brings to mind an image of an Irish farmhouse.

Lighthearted accessories add to the room's special charm. Particularly endearing are the toy horses parading across the mantel, the tiny wooden houses peeking from a shelf, the dolls sitting prettily on a bench, and the toy soldiers keeping watch at the window, *above.*

continued

Irish
Inspiration
(continued)

Like many country buffs, Mary Gilroy loves change. In her house, nothing stays the same for long, not even the color schemes. When the mood strikes her, she switches furnishings from one room to another, assuring visual variety.

Recently, she refined and "recolored" the rustic master bedroom, *right*, by adorning the bed with a "new" old Amish quilt, and topping the twig settee with an equally colorful appliquéd quilt and pillows. The bright hues of the fabrics offer lively contrast to barnwood paneling and pine plank floors.

Also new to the bedroom setting—but not to the house—is the painted dry sink, *above*, now put to work as a nightstand.

In the Country Spirit
Two-Part Harmony

Although Ron and Jean Dolan are relative newcomers to the world of collecting, they've more than made up for lost time. Not only have they filled their Georgian Revival house with a dazzling array of painted furniture and colorful kilim rugs, but they've done so in an enviably confident way.

The magical ease that marks the Dolans' decorating style didn't happen overnight. Like all neophyte collectors, they had to go through a period of looking and learning, making mistakes, and refining the eye. That process led them to a museum seminar on kilims, where the Dolans were smitten by the bright, painterly rugs. From there, says Ron, "it was an easy step" to painted furniture.

Today, assured in their tastes, the Dolans view collecting as a unifying process. Explains Ron, "Jean and I complement each other. The basic collecting urge comes from me; Jean refines it and puts it together."

The entry hall, *above*, with its grain-painted chest, is an elegant announcement of good things to come.   *continued*

Restrained and simple, the living room, *right,* demonstrates Jean's talent for creating a harmony of styles. The eye-catching olio includes a rust and turquoise Qashqai kilim rug, plump seating pieces, and a vibrant Star of Texas quilt fragment resting on the fireplace mantel. Ron and Jean's newest (and most treasured) acquisition is a circa 1840 painted wardrobe from Pennsylvania, placed in a commanding position between two windows.

The attention getter at the opposite end of the room, *above,* is a picture-perfect vignette featuring a painted barn louver from New England. At *right,* a mustard-painted Sheraton table shares the decorative spotlight with a colorful wall-hung kilim.

Two-Part Harmony
(continued)

A minor tug of war took place when the Dolans moved from Washington, D.C., to St. Louis in 1984. Jean, a sentimentalist, wanted all of their country furnishings to make the move, but Ron—a self-described "ruthless" weeder-outer—wanted to take just the best painted pieces and sell their oak. In the end, Jean agreed with Ron and saw the move as a chance to upgrade their painted furniture collection.

One of the few vestiges of the Dolans' "oak period" is the claw-and-ball dining table that now graces the dining room, *left.* Though less rare than the green-painted 1870s worktable in the kitchen, *above,* the golden oldie is no less loved.

continued

49

Backgrounds play a big role in the Dolans' decorating scheme. Before choosing a paint color or wall covering, the couple considers just what it is they're trying to show off, then proceeds from there. In the living room, walls were painted a neutral cream color so as not to compete with the colorful rugs, quilts, and painted furnishings. The quieter furnishings in the dining room were given zest by comb-painting the canvas walls in a rich shade of rust.

Another tactic was taken in the breakfast room, *right.* Here, an emerald green wall covering was chosen to sharply contrast with the delicate mustard tones of the stenciled Windsor chairs, the birch table, and the yellow ocher door hung as art.

The sun-room, *above,* with its pale yellow walls, exudes a summery feeling all year long.

continued

Unlike the downstairs, which was remodeled and formalized in the 1930s, the upstairs of the Dolans' 1904 house has never been touched. The original yellow pine floors are still intact, and the architecture is starkly simple.

Furnishings in all of the upstairs rooms, including the master bedroom, *left,* and the hallway, *above*, befit the unaffected country atmosphere. The 1820s chestnut-painted rope bed is one of the Dolans' favorite pieces, as is the folk art blanket chest at the foot of the bed.

Providing visual pleasure in the hallway is an old pine table with pencil-thin legs, topped with an unusual canvas goose decoy from North Carolina.

Home At Last

J ohn and Anne Houser are country buffs from way back. In their 20 years of marriage, they have lived in, restored, and redecorated no less than eight different houses, all of them in a classic country mien. Along the way, both Housers dabbled in buying and selling antiques, and John became known as a master stenciler.

But times—or at least the Housers—have changed, and the couple has grown restless with the look and life-style they once embraced. Their new approach to country living began with the purchase of a cedar-sided house, *right*—a contemporary shell filled with vintage surprises, *above.*

continued

S everal years ago, the Housers never would have dreamed that they'd sell their turn-of-the-century Victorian house and buy this one: A place with no "proper" front or back yard, no center hall floor plan, no separate living room or dining room. But far from being put off by these so-called negatives, the Housers were hooked. Indeed, when the real estate agent apologetically described the house as having just one big room and a kitchen downstairs, and two bedrooms upstairs, John said, "That's perfect. We'll be right over."

Why the about-face after spending so many years in large, traditional houses? "We were tired of taking care of space," says Anne. John adds, "At mid-life, you want something different."

Architectural change isn't the only kind the Housers have sought. Their approach to country has taken a new twist as well. In recent years, John—a Spanish teacher—has become a free-lance decorator, and his tastes have broadened considerably. Once enamored of a pure, rustic look, John today strives for "a mix of things. It's tedious to look at just one style and no others," he explains.

The great room, *left*, with its elegant English chintz fabrics and "anything goes" assortment of American and English antiques, captures the essence of the Housers' refreshing eclectic approach.   *continued*

Whereas one end of the great room is country cozy, the other end, *right*, is contemporary in mood. Here, windows soar two and a half stories, filling the room with light and affording a brilliant view of the woods and a meandering creek.

The sunny sitting area is furnished with a spirited amalgam of elements, including: a chinoiserie-patterned chintz sofa, a West Virginia painted cupboard, a pine blanket chest used as a coffee table, a handsome folk-art goose decoy, and a black painted American chair. Adding zing to the setting is an early 20th-century Turkish kilim rug, appropriately called a "dazzler." It's this kind of unexpected element that the Housers seek in redefining their approach to country.

Although they're trying to steer away from what John terms the "standard" country look, the Housers haven't spurned all forms of rusticity. Take the random-width wood floor, for example. John laid it himself using 1-inch-thick white pine boards imported to the Midwest from New Hampshire. Finished with linseed oil, the floor is not only handsome, but easy to maintain. Also rustic—but maybe not for long— are the hollow ceiling beams, original to the house. John presently is debating whether to paint the ersatz beams white.

continued

A iming for design diversity, the Housers have furnished the dining area with English fabrics, Spanish artwork, and a potpourri of American antiques. A rare Sheraton harvest table from New Hampshire is a beautiful presence. Surrounded by black-painted arrow-back chairs, the scrub-top table is centered on a trompe l'oeil marble floor, hand painted by John. The bordered motif defines the dining area and creates the feeling of a room within a room.

Placed in front of the balloon-shaded window is a delicate early 19th-century Pembroke table, painted in a mellow mahogany brown. To the right of the table is a painted Queen Anne blanket chest enhanced by a dome-topped document box and reproduction El Greco portrait.

continued

61

The man from whom the Housers bought the house not only built it himself, but designed it, too. His only failing—as far as John and Anne were concerned—was the kitchen; a dark little room, made even darker by its low ceiling and one tiny window. To remedy the situation, the Housers gutted the room and restyled it to their liking.

The result is a streamlined space, *right,* featuring white-painted cabinets, a butterscotch-colored pine floor, and matching pine countertops. Adding international flavor are colorful Mexican tiles used as a back-splash and an English chintz window valance trimmed in ribbon. In keeping room tradition, the remodeled kitchen opens to the dining and living area, *above.*

continued

Just off the brick-floored entrance hall, *above*, is the Housers' new master bedroom, *right*, formerly a garage. Distanced as it is from the main living area and the children's rooms upstairs, the beamed-ceiling bedroom is designed as an away-from-it-all oasis.

Unlike the rest of the house, the feeling here is decidedly Colonial. The bed—an exacting reproduction of a rare, early 19th-century tester bed—is topped with authentic hangings, handmade by Anne. The same blue-and-white Williamsburg colors used on the bed are repeated on the walls, enhancing the room's Colonial ambience.

New Country Style

Like America, country is a melting pot—an ever-changing mix of old and new influences, spiced with personal style. Fresh-faced, surprising, beautiful: This is country today.

New Country Style
Simply Beautiful

The Mrozinskis' living room (left) is as inviting as the California sunshine. Flanking a primitive bench, a pair of plump sofas wears French ticking, a crisp counterpoint to the muted color of a New England painted cupboard. Simple surroundings spotlight childhood collectibles, neatly nestled in shelves (above).

Lighthearted and extraordinarily personal, a new generation of country rooms succeeds on fresh colors, clean lines, and the judicious display of treasures. In their California home, owners Paul and Sharon Mrozinski invoked these qualities to create a haven washed by the sun and warmed by a fine collection of Americana. Sharon, an antiques dealer, brought to the home her love of primitives and pine. Paul, an artist, contributed a penchant for clean-lined furnishings and the drama of white backdrops.

continued

Simply Beautiful

(continued)

B ecause the Mrozinski home is blessed with a rural location and enviable views, its generous windows remain unadorned. By day, the dining room's English pine table and farm-style chairs compose an unpretentious setting for family meals and casual get-togethers. But, as night approaches and shadows lengthen, the plain furnishings take on a distinctive sculptural quality, adding a degree of drama to the room's inherent hospitality.

The Mrozinskis' spare-is-better philosophy plays beautifully in the dining room (right), where they invited nature to lend a hand in their decorating. With a wealth of windows, dining in this sun-drenched spot is almost al fresco.

The mammoth pine table originally was fitted with a deep skirt that left little legroom; a skilled cabinetmaker remade the table for dining. The couple added folk art accents and rag runners, then settled back to let the California sun do the rest.

Soft and Inviting

Dressed-up country rooms embrace life's simple pleasures: pretty patterns, soft color and lines, and a touch of sentiment. Easygoing and elegant, the sitting room, *left,* is a rich mix of English and American, folk and formal, all dulcified with garden-fresh prints and a soothing tint of peach.

*Owners Barbara and Arthur McDonnell brought a soft touch to their porch-turned-sitting-room **(left)**. Nestled in a generous bay, a chintz-dressed love seat keeps company with fine antiques, including a 17th-century Windsor chair and* *an English grandmother's clock. The lace at the windows was quickly aged by steeping the valances in weak tea. In an adjoining nook **(above)**, a honey-hued Welsh dresser is propped with personal treasures.*

73

New Country Style
A Personal Mix

A mong the most enchanting homes are those auto-graphed with the owner's personal signature. With a spirited mix of family heirlooms, mementos, and collectibles, rooms emerge warm and welcoming, in true country style.

Such is the home of Joyce and Donald Gair, collectors who followed their hearts in decorating their suburban living room, *right.* The couple created a friendly focus with floor-to-ceiling bookshelves, then anchored the seating area with an old deacon's bench that they bought for $10 and rehabilitated. A congenial cast of old and unusual furnishings imbues the room with vintage character.

*With accents found from Maine to Mexico—and antiques that hail from old England and New, the Gairs' living room **(right and above)** is full of conversation pieces. Linen dresses up the hand-me-down sofa and wing chair, and new cushions soften old spindle-back chairs. An antique English butler's tray **(above)** boasts a Mexican box filled with Donald Gair's boyhood tops.*

74

New Country Style
Farmhouse Memories

The legacy of rural roots and simpler times, farmhouse furniture, with its honest beauty and clean lines, enjoys enduring appeal in today's pared interiors. For many devotees, these pure and practical pieces will forever be the essence of country style. The convivial dining room, *left,* takes heart from straightforward American furnishings and the owners' deft display of collectibles.

The farmstead dining room (left) recaptures the country hospitality of generations past. Be it family dinners or a neighborly get-together, the center attraction is a Shaker-simple walnut table, its vintage character the work of a modern-day craftsman. Edging it is a quartet of century-old pine chairs, auction finds the owner restored with newly woven cotton-tape seats. Homespun accents include a folk crafter's weather vane and a hooked rug mounted on black canvas.

77

New Country Style
A Blend of Old and New

*It's hard to tell where old ends and new begins in this restored, 18th-century keeping room (**left**). An antique English trunk serves as a coffee table, but the pine end tables are new, hand-crafted pieces. Picking up on tradition, the sumptuous seating pieces wear deep skirts and a pretty, white-on-white version of a colonial flame-stitch pattern.*

Above, a new high-back chair blends seamlessly with an antique game table and bench.

When the mellow woods and aged artifacts of country meet the cool, economical lines of contemporary, what emerges are rooms that crackle with character.

In the keeping room, *left,* modular white seating and stark white walls provide the crispness of contemporary styling; a worldly assemblage of country pieces contributes the warmth of tradition. Set in a restored, circa-1730 New England colonial, the mix spans the ages beautifully.

In furnishing the home, the owners wisely blended, as well as contrasted, old and new: Fine handcrafted wood pieces commingle with authentic pine antiques, and even the contemporary seating pieces feature traditional detailing.

79

New Country Style
Accent on Comfort

Comfort is a hallmark of the country life-style—and the country home. Cares ebb and spirits recharge in rooms that radiate the warmth of mellow woods, no-fuss furnishings, and finely wrought reminders of yesteryear.

The 1890s farmhouse, *left,* sums up the appeal of relaxed surroundings. After renovation exposed a spectacular fieldstone fireplace, the homeowners made it the heart of a gathering spot for family and friends. Sink-down seating, easy-care fabrics, and well-worn tables and chests issue an invitation to linger.

*Comfort comes first in this living room (**left**). Simply styled love seats, pulled up to the hearth, sport a robust red plaid fabric as irresistible as a favorite flannel shirt. The old American pine table already shows timeworn character, so there's no need to fret over today's scratches.*

Avid collectors, the owners fitted the fireplace with a rough-hewn pine slab, which now holds a charming lineup of mugs and an earthy jug.

81

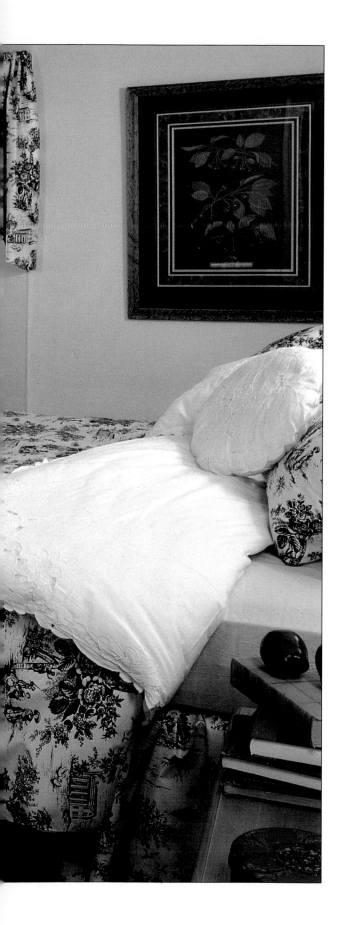

Old-World Romance

Beautifully nostalgic, the bedroom (left and above) carries on the best pampering traditions. The marble-topped fruitwood dressing table is a French antique, teamed with a new wicker chair. The metal bed is queen-size.

Hanging on the wall is an antique English lavabo. In days past, servants would fill the tank, mounted on a tall plank, with water, so the fastidious English could take a morning scrub.

Dressed in luxurious linens and set with the quaint flourishes of yesterday, country rooms can summon a special sense of intimacy and old-world charm. Unabashedly sentimental, such exquisite spaces soothe and satisfy with an alluring emphasis on softness and comfort.

The bedroom, *left,* set in an 18th-century colonial home, borrows its elegant air from continental antiques, fine reproductions, and elegant fabrics. Its centerpiece is an ornate, black metal fence bed, *above,* so called because its curlicues and brass finials recall Victorian wrought-iron fencing. A delightful, black-and-white toile fabric—an adaption of an old French print—dresses the bed and window.

Spiced With Color

Muted buttermilk hues and hushed earth tones, once the hallmark of heritage interiors, now have company on the country palette. Today, country rooms embrace a full spectrum of color, from the bold primaries of old quilts to the subtle, soft shadings of a cottage garden. There's growing evidence that this yearning for color is more than a latter-day trend. Researchers analyzing chips of antique paint have discovered that early American homes were much more vividly colored than once believed. The best reason for using color isn't historical accuracy, however: It's the exuberance that confident color can bring to favorite rooms.

The owner of this old mill home (above) satisfied his yen for color by brushing aged chairs with cheery yellow and painting a kitchen wall a soft shade of pumpkin.

A collection of red-and-white quilts inspired the warmly colored guest room (right). The richness of red is astutely tempered with simple furnishings and soft, lacy accents.

Eclectic and Inviting

Refusing to be bound by period or pedigree of furnishings, innovative country rooms achieve singular beauty with a sprightly blend of styles. A master of the unexpected, designer Alexander Baer packed personality into the living room of his century-old farmhouse by combining the best of English traditions with contemporary livability. Wrapped in springtime colors and punctuated with collectibles from around the world, the living room exudes a comfort and ease that is the essence of the country life-style.

Fluid in design and free in spirit, Baer's farmhouse living room is a pleasing primer on eclectic style—as well as country comfort. Says Baer, "There is nothing in the house that you can't put your feet on."

Bathed in sunshine, the corner (left) has a decidedly English flavor, with a lively mix of patterned

fabrics and a collection of Staffordshire figures. The living room (above) mixes purely country pieces, such as the mellow pine cupboard, with the natural textures of bamboo and wicker. Gilt-framed artwork and a lacquered screen add a touch of the refined.

From Modern-Day Hands

Handmade objects are a hallmark of the country home. Today's artists and crafters keep alive the tradition of the handmade—proving that pride and imagination endure.

Furniture Of Fancy

Fine furniture is sometimes said to have character: honest lines, distinctive wood, assured style. But only rarely does it have true personality, whereby the wit, vision, and charm of its maker are revealed as well.

Such is the work of Tommy Simpson, who is so magically in tune with wood that he can make a sunflower sprout on a chair and antlers spring from a clock. In the fanciful form of his furniture shines the spirit of an artist determined to share the twinkle in his eye.

Tommy has been "making things," as he modestly terms it,

almost his entire life, and is formally trained as an artist. Although he works easily in a variety of art forms—from metalworking to painting and sculpture—he finds woodworking particularly satisfying.

"Furniture making is a discipline on a human scale," he

says. "You can acquire your materials, execute your ideas, and feel a real sense of accomplishment—all within your own length of concentration and passion."

A sense of passion as well as a sense of humor is inherent in Tommy's work. Indeed, what makes his pieces so intriguing is his ability to see beyond the rules of traditional furniture forms and introduce fresh, unexpected, and often witty elements. "Everything I make is a

continued

Tommy Simpson (above) lives and works surrounded by the handmade. Amid odd-shaped mittens and miniature furniture is his armoire (opposite), made of bird's-eye maple, cherry, and English oak. Tommy's mother made the needlepoint cover for her son's playful *version of the Queen Anne chair.*
The tall-case clock (right) borrows its antlers and bark face from rustic adirondack furniture, and its playful styling from Tommy's vivid imagination. It also gives a new twist to the Latin phrase for "time flies."

'salad'—of ideas, people, situations, historical references,"
he says.

On his clock, for instance, he merged two stylistic opposites into a delightful hybrid. The staid proportions of an 18th-century tall-case clock were mated with the rough wood, horns, and rustic feel of 19th-century adirondack-style camp furniture for the sheer fun of chemistry. "It was like bringing two people together at a party," says Tommy. "You can never tell what's going to happen, but there's no reason not to try."

This willingness to try new forms—to "stay open to the possibilities," as Tommy puts it—results in furniture that is hard to categorize, but easy to love. Some pieces celebrate the

continued

Above: One-of-a-kind rockers exemplify Tommy's sense of humor. The sunflower rocker, of walnut and maple, sports cartoonlike legs. The American Indian piece features an inlaid heart and stars on the feet.
Right: Shapely dining chairs gather around a table crafted from English oak slabs. Tommy named the chairs in pairs: For instance, the one inscribed "Butter" goes with "Snow," a play on the "Butter Snow" variety of corn.

material itself: His four-poster, for example, has head- and footboards constructed from rough oak slabs that "make you aware of where wood comes from." Other times, decorative elements drive the design.

To tweak the eye and the ear, Tommy often carves favorite words and poems into the decoration as well. Across the top of a favorite armoire is an example of what he calls "casserole writing"—a tasty, if nonsensical, mix of musical words like "hollyhock" and "dumpling."

Traditional American design themes emerge in many of

Tommy's pieces. A set of dining chairs borrows one wide arm from the Windsor writing-arm chairs of the 18th and 19th centuries; another chair takes the flowing cabriole legs of the Queen Anne style to comically sinuous extremes.

No object is too humble for Tommy's attention. Brooms sprout handles sprinkled with inlaid stars; banisters sway as nimbly as flower stems; stools sport carved legs or seats.

"I do this (work) because I can't help it," says Tommy simply. "The best expression of 'me' is my best work. I think the quality comes through because it is so close to what I am. And maybe if people have the chance to see a person doing a certain thing that they love, it will give them ideas to explore in their own selves."

The canopy bed **(opposite),** *made of the same English oak as the dining table, takes its slender posts from antique pencil-post beds. A sunflower bedstand grows nearby.*

Banisters in the stairwell **(above)** *interpret the natural, undulating stems of flowers.*

The household drudgery of sweeping is lightened by the trio of brooms **(above),** *each with a decorative handle. Even utilitarian stools are given new personality in Tommy's varied renditions* **(left).** *Often made of wood scraps, they nonetheless show individuality. Each has shaped seats and sculpted legs and stretchers.*

Modern-Day Hands
Woven Artistry

For weaver Missy Stevens, the loom is more than a tool of industry: It's an artist's easel, where fabric, design, and imagination meet and intertwine.

Drawn to both painting and fabrics, Missy combines both interests by creating one-of-a-kind pictures on the loom. Under her inspired touch, weavings as functional as tea cozies and rag rugs become soft canvases on which she expresses her outlook on color, composition, and the country life.

For her palette, Missy uses strips torn from old cotton corduroy pants, a material that yields a uniquely rich and soft texture. Just as importantly, slight color variations from piece to piece allow Missy to achieve near-infinite nuances in tone, replicating the irregularities of old hand-dyed pieces.

Missy began weaving rag rugs in 1976. Her early designs were very simple stripes and checks; for added decoration, she always included a folkish

continued

A pair of pillows (left), teamed here with a tweedy wool throw, were woven as Valentine's Day gifts for a friend. Missy's superb sense of color and whimsy are apparent in her tea cozies (below), which often are made of end pieces left from larger projects. The cat cozy sports yarn whiskers, rakish ears, and a jaunty bow tie.

Departing from her usual practice of using strips from old corduroy pants, Missy wove this softly colored rag carpet (opposite) from modern yard goods, which yield a flatter texture.

Because of its extra-large size—about 14x17 feet—Missy created five panels, then tacked them together on her bedroom floor.

heart in one corner. These inlaid hearts, pieced over rag strips in the body of the rug, led to more complicated pictures. "That I could make pictures on the loom is what really got my interest," says Missy. "The pictures got bigger and bigger until they took over the whole rug."

Surrounded by baskets of corduroy strips, Missy weaves her designs on two large floor looms. The motifs on rag rugs, throws, and pillow covers are devised directly on the loom. For more intricate pieces, she creates inlaid motifs with the guidance of stencillike patterns. Border panels are woven separately, then joined with braids.

Underlying the design of Missy's weavings is her deep attachment to things country.

"I draw on the things I love," she says, "and I have always loved the trees and gardens and birds, the ocean and the woods. The natural world is very nourishing to me."

Missy Stevens (above) creates her weavings in a Connecticut country workshop.

Her two simply patterned pillows (left) are decorated with braided trim and her signature inlaid hearts—a universal symbol she feels shares the folkish flavor of her weavings.

The ponies cavorting among the moon and stars on the rug (right) were inspired by the dreamlike motifs frequently seen in southwestern Indian art.

Modern-Day Hands

Country In the Round

Sally Cammack (top) etches her folkish designs on dried gourds with a woodburning pen. The gourd above bears Sally's bird's-eye views of village life. As "my form of graffiti," Sally included her maiden name on the "Powell's Dairy" wagon.

The varied shapes of gourds, as seen in those opposite, make the artistic process more challenging.

From the fruits of a country garden, Kentucky folk artist Sally Cammack serves up a slice of the country life. Painting gourds with carefully observed and delightfully rendered scenes of rural living, Sally creates miniature worlds that brim with warmth and small-town humor.

Sally's decorative gourds draw on two folk traditions. Her skillful painting is inspired by the naive landscapes of 19th-century American folk artists. And, like many folk artists before her, Sally has chosen an alternative to canvas for her art. Her media—gourds—have been used and decorated in North and South American Indian cultures for centuries.

Sally's mother-in-law discovered painted gourds on a trip to Peru in 1981, and shared with Sally her method for re-creating them. Fascinated, Sally began to experiment on gourds she had saved from autumn. Using a woodburning pen, she sketched simple patterns on the gourd surface, then colored the patterns with felt-tip markers. A crafts-shop owner who saw her work suggested that Sally try composing entire scenes.

Suddenly, Sally found her niche. Her love of small-town life and her pleasure in drawing and fine detail all came together in gourds—from huge "bushel" gourds the size of bushel baskets, to dainty egg-shaped ones.

continued

*A coat of varnish protects the finished gourds **(left)**, whose color will continue to mellow with time. Egg-sized gourds, like those **below, left,** call for simple motifs, including a sly fox astride a hound. **Right:** Gourds fill a pie safe with country pleasures.*

The path from garden to finished gourd is an arduous one. Sally buys her gourds from country gardeners, selecting fruits with smooth, uniform skins. While the gourds dry, which takes from three months to a year, a shell of mold forms over their skins. The mold has to be scrubbed off to yield a hard, workable surface. Even then, "you can never tell how the gourd will take color," says Sally, who now uses watercolor pens instead of felt-tip markers to "paint" the scenes.

Although all of Sally's designs are original, certain themes recur: country villages, modest farmhouses, bustling school yards. For inspiration, Sally draws on scenes she sees from the windows of her home, set in the rolling hills of Kentucky, and on scenes she conjures up with a daydreamer's eye. Her nostalgic villages, for example, are reminiscent of her own small hometown; the dashing fox hunts she portrays, with riders in traditional scarlet coats, are a bluegrass tradition.

Far from frozen time-capsule views, Sally's depictions of country life are rich, exciting, and full of humor. Dogs playfully steal clothes from the swimming hole, or tug laundry from a basket; young boys eavesdrop from the treetops as girls whisper their secrets below. On the gourds, as in life, says Sally, "The more people look, the more they see."

Modern-Day Hands
Etched In Clay

Redware pottery has been made in America since the days of the earliest settlements. Encouraged by abundant clay deposits along the Eastern seaboard, early craftsmen turned out everything from bowls and jugs to tiles and whistles. Although fancier earthenwares eclipsed redware's popularity in the 18th century, no pottery has ever been able to match its burnished, elemental beauty.

German settlers in the Mid-Atlantic region were especially gifted in working with redware, and today Jeff White carries on their craft in the heart of Pennsylvania-German country.

Jeff began collecting redware as a teen, long before he had an inkling that pottery would become his profession. A few art courses in college convinced him to concentrate on ceramics and its chemistry. "I'm fascinated by the art *and* science of ceramics," he says.

Today, Jeff divides his work between reproduction of traditional pieces and creation of his own original designs. His range of pottery includes many of the centuries-old forms—platterlike chargers, jugs and crocks, fruit-shaped coin banks, and bird and animal figurines.

All the pieces are thrown on a potter's wheel, except plates, which are formed by draping rolled clay over a completed mold. *continued*

Craftsman Jeff White (top) carries on the tradition of early American potters in creating redware, the country's first domestic ceramics. Living in the heart of Pennsylvania-German country, *Jeff has adopted many of that region's characteristic redware forms and decorative styles. His plate (above) reproduces an original sgraffito, or etched, design now in the New York* *Metropolitan Museum of Art. The handmade cupboard (opposite) displays Jeff's range of talent in clay, from large plates and jugs to small animals and fruit-shaped coin banks.*

The pieces then are decorated, with traditional colored glazes, like manganese and iron for sparkling black, copper carbonate for green, and clay slip for yellow.

The special challenge of working in redware is expressing new ideas within this limited palette. "Redware forces you to work harder to be fresh because of the available colors and materials," Jeff says.

To make the craft his own, Jeff produces many complicated sgrafitto pieces, which involves etching designs in a layer of light clay that coats the redware surface to create a contrast of light and dark. In addition to his controlled reproductions of Pennsylvania-German motifs, Jeff creates looser renditions of horses, farmhouses, and animals on his sgrafitto plates.

On crocks, cups, and other utensils, Jeff sometimes ventures into even bolder new design, pouring or sponging on color for an element of surprise.

Three of the antique pieces in Jeff's long-standing collection are the flowerpot, pitcher, and crock, (above). The pitcher, stamped with tiny stars, is exceptionally fine and rare.

To brighten and enliven the dull brick-red clay, Jeff continues to use the same glazes that colonial potters did. Although Jeff enjoys the discipline of making exact reproductions, "I also want to express my own ideas," he says. The result is adventurous and original designs like those at right.

Sculptor In Wood

With his sensitive modeling of human and animal figures, woodcarver William Jauquet elevates the old country pastime of whittling to the realm of folk sculpture.

A self-taught craftsman, Bill began putting his natural abilities into action around 1980,

when his wife requested a carved swan for her antiques shop. That first simple piece launched Bill's new career as creator and caretaker of a varied menagerie.

Like generations of folk carvers before him, Bill became captivated by the individuality, shapes, and antics of the animal world. Soon, sculpted cows, roosters, pigs, and giraffes were springing from the cedar logs in his rural Wisconsin studio. Many of his favorite pieces are horses, finely wrought reminders of an Arabian Bill once

continued

*Opposite, top:
Working with a
rasp, carver Bill
Jauquet wrings
flowing lines from
blocks of wood in
his Wisconsin
studio. His love of
animals, horses in
particular, is
apparent in the
sensitive rendering
of this quartet
(opposite,
bottom). Their
gentle faces and
graceful poses, each
unique, reflect the
essential equine
spirit.*

*Inspired by
Noah's arks of
yesteryear, one of
the few playthings
children were
allowed on the
Sabbath, Bill's
version of the classic
"Sunday toy"
(above) measures
42 inches long and
38 inches high. It
is populated by
some 20 pairs of
animals, from tiny
birds to trumpeting
elephants, along
with Noah and his
family (right).*

Sculptor In Wood

(continued)

owned. "I've always loved horses," says Bill, "They are one of the few subjects in which I can combine power and elegance."

Often depicted in close association with man, Bill's horses bear signs of his deep admiration for their free spirit and loyalty. In his work "Day's End," for example, a spry horse faithfully pulls home a wagonload of workmen who slump motionless from fatigue.

Bill strives less to define his subjects realistically than to imply their natures artistically. A young cyclist with a piglet tucked under his arm, for instance, is the essence of boyhood pranks. Over the years, Bill's carvings have grown more stylized, with subtly suggested details conveying the theme.

The unstudied charm of his carvings derives in part from his working methods. Uncomfortable with sketching, Bill starts the creative process directly with the wood. After roughly shaping laminated blocks of white pine with a band saw, Bill slowly forms his subjects with two inexpensive rasps from a farm store. "They were supposed to be defective, but I probably still do 75 percent of my work with them," he says.

Such a spontaneous approach ensures that no two pieces are ever alike, as do Bill's various finishing methods. Combinations of sealants, distressing techniques, wax, and paints make each creation a unique expression of the carver's craft.

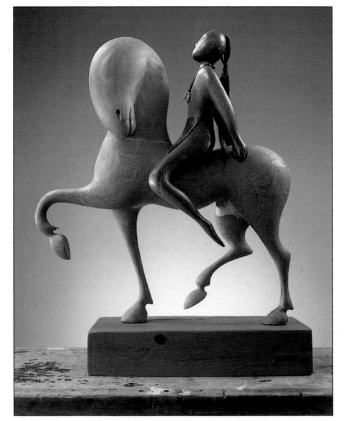

Bill's interest in patriotic subjects has taken the form of an Abe Lincoln whirligig and George Washington on horseback (top left). The general waves a leather flag dotted with 13 stars and holds a leather rein, which Bill fashioned as the finishing touch. The mane and tail are genuine horsehair.

This serene and dignified Indian figure (bottom left) shows the progression of Bill's carvings toward increased stylization. The lack of clearly defined detail invites the viewer's personal interpretation. Though Bill is serious about his craft, he does not restrict himself to serious subjects. The piece (opposite) based on a lighthearted suggestion from a neighbor, puts an unlikely twist on the sentimental theme of a boy and his pet.

Heart of The South

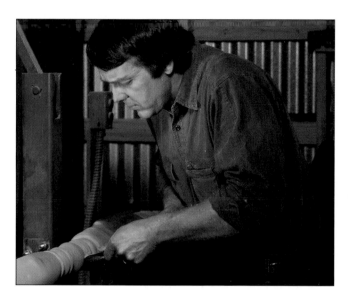

A turn-of-the-century lathe, along with other old tools, helps cabinetmaker Sam Jackson (above) create furniture adapted from designs of the 1830s to 1850s. His specialty is working with native heart pine, salvaged from old buildings.

The armoire (left) features raised-panel doors and is scaled for today's homes. It's shown with Sam's huntboard, a distinctive Southern variation on the dining room sideboard.

For Georgia craftsman Sam Jackson, furniture making is an affair of the heart—heart pine, that is. Dedicated to preserving the tradition of 19th-century Southern furniture, Jackson embraces not only its craftsmanship and subdued style, but also the special native wood from which it was made.

Along with mahogany and walnut, heart pine—a hard, close-grained wood—was used in the huntboards, cellarettes, and planter's desks typical of the South. Today, the slow-maturing, long-leaf yellow pine is no longer forested, and the supply is limited. "There always was and always will be beautiful walnut, cherry, and mahogany, but there will never be more heart pine," Sam says sadly.

continued

113

Heart of
The South
(continued)

Sam believes that the only way to save the precious resource, which he salvages from buildings slated for destruction, is to recycle it into furniture for coming generations. "I'm proud to be leaving something," says Sam, "instead of taking away."

The son of a lumberman, Sam learned the rudiments of cabinetmaking at age 12. By constantly studying antique pieces, Sam educated himself about regional design and refined his sense of style.

Such disciplined training has allowed him to reinterpret 19th-century furniture rather than merely duplicate it. In composing new pieces, Sam may borrow a leg style from one piece, moldings from another, turnings from yet another. The result is beds, tables, chairs, chests, cupboards, and other pieces with authentic 19th-century lines, but with personally crafted style and contemporary scale.

In working with such venerable wood—some of the heart pine Sam uses is 400- to 500-year-old virgin growth—the cabinetmaker relies on the tools and techniques of the past. A lathe from 1901 turns handsome bedposts, and the saws and planes that shape the milled boards are hand-powered. Mortise-and-tenon and dovetail joints, along with square pegs and hand-forged, rosehead nails are used to fasten the furniture the same way it was done in the 1800s.

The four-poster (left) combines elements from four beds and two tables; it's teamed with Sam's plain-style, drop-leaf table and a blanket chest.

The silver chest (above and below) shows off hand-etched hardware and a silky finish. Sam rubs his pieces with up to 12 coats of lacquer.

Worked In Willow

The cool, comfortable willow furniture of Monte Lindsley whispers of Victorian society, mountain resorts, and the fanciful twig pieces popular in the late 19th century. But even more clearly, his furniture speaks of nature itself: The exuberant shapes and colors of Monte's rustic chairs, rockers, and settees could only spring from an outdoor-lover, with an eye for the nuances of the wild.

A former professional forester and landscaper, Monte gives the impression of a man completely at ease with his environment. "My designs are influenced by nature and the stimulation it gives me," he says. Indeed, the looping arcs of his chair backs are so delicate that they seem to have been traced by birds in flight. And the rich colors of the pieces—from pale straw to deep garnet—reflect the ever-changing palette of the woods.

Monte begins by harvesting choice shoots from Washington's swamplands, and bending

continued

*Furniture maker Monte Lindsley **(above, right)** secures arcing willow shoots onto a sturdy frame, letting his eye guide the design. A man attuned to nature, Monte built "floating islands"—shallow boxes filled with soil and planted with native trees—on his ponds in Washington **(above, left)**.*

*The intertwining loops on Monte's furniture **(right)** recall bentwood pieces made by rural artisans at the turn of the century. The painted chair and natural bark settee **(right)** reflect the colors of the woods.*

Worked
In Willow

(continued)

and stretching them inch by inch to render them supple. The self-taught artist, who studied photos of old willow furniture, then forms his signature hoops around a sturdy, straight twig frame until arms, backs, and seats emerge. With no pattern to guide him, Monte relies on experience to wrest a satisfying design from the wiry material.

Nature supplies the final touch: Finished pieces cure in the sunshine for several weeks to achieve their final color.

*Willow is a hardwood that becomes stronger and more beautiful with age. Monte sprays his finished pieces with varnish, then lets them "season" in the sun for several weeks. The result is bark that can cure to a ruddy chestnut brown, like the sofa at **left**. Other pieces are peeled and allowed to mellow to a pale straw color, like the work **above**. Its dynamic, sweeping lines lend the piece a sense of movement, even though it is sitting still.*

Modern-Day Hands
Buying Crafts

With the renewed interest in America's heritage, modern-day country crafts are available almost everywhere. You can buy crafts in galleries and small shops, through fairs and exhibitions, and directly from artisans. But buying crafts is much like buying antiques: You'll fare better if you educate yourself first.

Although you should always buy what you like, you'll shop with a more discriminating eye if you've done some research. Books at your library or bookstore can help you get a feel for the elements that constitute quality work. Also, many national craft associations publish magazines that detail outstanding works in each medium.

Where to See Crafts

Of course, seeing fine crafts firsthand is the best way to refine your tastes. More and more American museums devote space to crafts. Three—the American Craft Museum in New York, the Renwick Gallery in Washington, D. C., and the Craft and Folk Art Museum in Los Angeles—are devoted primarily to crafts; these institutions often sponsor touring exhibits throughout the country.

Local and regional craft fairs offer a convenient, and pleasurable, way to stalk your favorite crafts. Craft fairs give you a chance to browse at your own pace and to ask plenty of questions. If you find craftspeople whose works interest you, don't hesitate to ask about their experience, training, and techniques.

The quality of work you'll find at fairs varies. Fairs organized by state or regional craft guilds generally promise high-quality handcrafts, because each piece must meet the guild's standards of excellence. Juried shows, where participants are screened by a panel, also may offer a higher quality of work.

American Craft Enterprises (P.O. Box 10, New Paltz, NY 12561), a nonprofit group, sponsors a preeminent, annual series of juried shows, in Baltimore, New York City, Minneapolis-St. Paul, San Francisco, and Springfield, Massachusetts. These shows tend to feature contemporary craft styles, offering a tantalizing glimpse at new techniques and design ideas.

Many craftspeople sell their work primarily—or exclusively—through galleries. If you're a serious collector, a gallery can be your best ally: In addition to displaying crafts, gallery owners often have slides of additional pieces and perhaps can guide you to a special work or artisan. *American Craft,* the magazine of the nonprofit American Craft Council, publishes a national listing of craft-oriented galleries.

Commissioning Crafts

If you can't find just the right piece for sale, you can explore two other options: special orders and commissions. *Special orders* involves buying duplicate pieces after having seen a prototype—a set of chairs or glasses, for instance. A *commission* entails working directly with an artisan to have a work designed and made especially for you—anything from a stenciled floorcloth to a set of dining room furniture.

No matter what the size of your commission, a few guidelines apply. First, you should feel totally comfortable with the artisan and his or her style and level of skill. It's also important to feel comfortable talking with the person: You need to clearly communicate your needs and wants, and to discuss freely ideas for the project. Talk budget right from the outset.

Finally, insist on a written agreement defining the scope of the project, the timetable, and the terms. Customarily, you'll be asked to deposit one-third of the price when you place the commission. In complicated commissions, you may be asked to approve a preliminary design and to make an interim payment at that point.

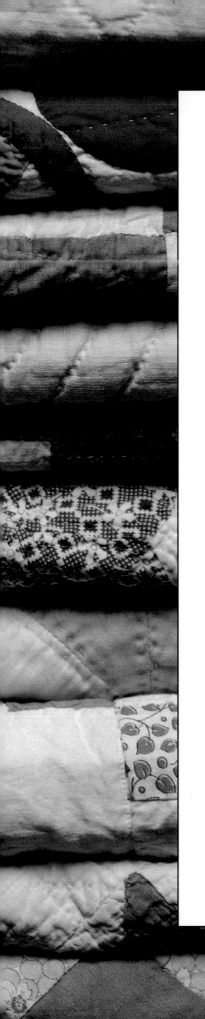

The Collector's Art

Collecting "country" is a passion, but displaying it is an art. Country collectibles—fine antiques or humble, everyday objects— are best honored by settings that show off their character.

The Collector's Art
Accent
An Entry

Collectibles extend country character to every corner of a house, beginning right inside the front door. A foyer filled with objects lovingly gathered over time issues an especially warm greeting. It not only welcomes visitors to a home, it offers them a peek into the heart.

Simple but striking, this entry (far left) sums up its owner's love of warmth and subtlety. An 1815 cupboard imparts a cozy glow, rain or shine. Showcased against new windows and quarry tile, a worn bench and a lineup of crocks enhance the homey mood.

A blending of seemingly incompatible items gives the stairway (top, left) one-of-a-kind personality. The dainty doll, fanciful majolica, and delicate artwork represent the collecting interests of one spouse; the geometric rug and Amish quilt demonstrate the bold design preferred by the other.

A sculptural, antique tricycle, stacked blocks, and a dimensional quilt (bottom, left) reflect this owner's eye for childlike whimsy and pure, graphic lines.

The Collector's Art
Show Off Simply

Fine collectibles, like fine art, deserve center stage. By keeping the backgrounds simple and groupings concise, the owners of the dining room, *right,* let the character of their collections shine through.

Bob and Patty Weiner are avid treasure hunters who can lay claim to a wealth of country artifacts. In this room, however, they wisely restrained themself to one major display—prized pieces of majolica, nestled into a scrubbed pine hutch. Old baskets and American folk art play a supporting role, reinforcing the room's understated, rustic quality.

Patty Weiner owns more than 200 pieces of majolica in all, but limits her dining room display **(right)** *primarily to bread trays and plates. She is particularly intrigued by American pieces, which are more rustic than their European counterparts. The brilliantly colored, lead-glazed earthware was introduced in England in the mid-1800s, and enjoyed a 50-year reign of popularity.*

Create Character

Collections can be memorable for the mood they set. Indeed, the most intriguing collections often are those bound not by style or period, but by the special vision of the collector. For toy-lover Carolyn Fishman, the vision is one of pure childhood wonderment.

It would be easy to mistake Carolyn Fishman's living room (below and opposite) for a nursery. In a way, it is—but only for adults. A collector since her teens,

Carolyn has used her love of all things childlike to set the room's happy tone.

Carolyn's collection spans the oceans and the centuries, but each object reflects youthful innocence.

Near the bay window (opposite), an early Victorian hobby horse from England joins with a tin soldier and a delightful birdcage to awaken a dull corner. On the pine worktable, German wind-up toys play in the yard of an antique dollhouse.

Fireside (below) is home for a menagerie of animals. A dappled horse from Maine appears to stare at a modern-day wooden cat with a mouse in its paws. Across the room, wagonloads of cuddly teddy bears appeal to the child within.

Call On Color

F ew country lovers can resist a "find": a bargain quilt, spirited folk art, a proud piece of painted furniture. The challenge is making it all work together once it gets home. In this pair of bedrooms, common denominators of color and pattern do the trick.

Cool and serene, this timeless bedroom (**above**) gets its snug appeal from a simple color scheme and a blend of classic geometric patterns.

The blue-and-white quilts and coverlet establish the room's scheme, and another quilt, draped over the camelback sofa, adds a dash of red. The 19th-century hooked rugs relate beautifully, because each was worked with lots of crisp white and accents of blue and red. Even the antique furnishings in the room share kindred, honey hues.

The same common-denominator principles create an entirely different look in this rustic retreat (**opposite**), where color and pattern set a lively mood.

Golden tones unify the bench, chair, and shutters; a darker brown unifies the primitive blanket chests, which double as bedside tables.

The rug, quilt, and wall hanging, too, are happily married with related blue tones and repeated diamond patterns.

The crowning burst of color: bright red shams that pick up a hue from the quilt.

The Collector's Art
Flavor a Kitchen

Kitchens are a natural gathering place for people and things, and there always seems to be room "for just one more." Though organized displays will fend off clutter, kitchens are a place where rules can be relaxed, feet propped on chairs, and homey groupings allowed to roost undisturbed.

The clean, sleek finishes of contemporary kitchens are a perfect foil for country collectibles. In this town-house galley **(opposite)**, a row of folk art houses forms a friendly country lane above the cabinet tops. A folk art dog watches—gargoylelike—over the scene.

The honeycombed storage system **(above)** is the soul of organization. Each cubbyhole was made to measure for the trinkets, treasures, or essentials it stores. Kindred colors make the effect especially pleasing.

Made to last, kitchen collectibles never go out of style or use. The gathering of well-worn (and still used) bowls and utensils **(right)** is unstudied, but the graduated sizes and related colors give it order. The ruffle-capped window helps frame the composition.

The Collector's Art
Group with Confidence

Time-honored accessories help create the nostalgic mood of country schemes, especially when they are arranged in vignettes that delight the eye and tug at the heartstrings. Arranging picture-perfect groupings is a matter of exercising a good eye—and mastering a few basic techniques of artful display. *continued*

In the same way that an area rug can anchor and unify a furniture grouping, a large-scale wall accent can pull together an artful arrangement of small collectibles. Instead of floating in space, this homespun mélange of well-worn woods, cloth dolls, and a mini Noah's Ark (opposite) is framed securely by a bold Roman Candle quilt. In addition to the quilt, the variety of scale lends interest to the mix.

Great groupings require balance, but not necessarily symmetry. These avian artifacts (top right) are a case in point. Instead of being centered above the dry sink, the yellow tiered cage from the 1890s hangs to one side and is counterbalanced by three smaller cages to the right. Even the painted chair, set opposite the large yellow cage, helps level the scales visually.

The beauty of simple, functional elements is the tie that binds the pieces in this cozy corner (bottom right). A Shaker-style desk— elegant in its purity of line—anchors a mix of Amish clothing "framed" by a kindred peg rack.

Group with Confidence

(continued)

*Few hearts can resist the appeal of teddies, one of country's favorite collectibles **(top, right)**. Potentially "lost," not to mention lonely, if spread out around the house, this family of huggable stuffed bears snuggles happily together amid the soft folds of an aging quilt.*

*Displayed against the delicate, weblike designs of antique lace, a collection of snuff boxes **(bottom, right)** encourages passersby to stop and linger for a moment. The matte texture of the lace, as well as its light hue, help to play up the sheen of the polished wood and metal beauties. Snuff boxes, small, decorative containers filled with aromatic tobacco, were carried by gentlemen—and sometimes ladies— in the 17th, 18th, and 19th centuries.*

Toy enthusiast Judy Aikawa describes collecting as "an addiction, an obsession." Yet she finds the discipline to present her treasures in delightful bites, as in the open cupboard **(below)**. Generous spacing gives each toy room to shine, with top billing going to a "very old" wagon drawn by a hide-covered horse. A comb-backed Windsor chair and sculptural stack of firkins meld the cupboard into a larger composition, and a Noah's Ark watercolor winks at its real-life counterpart.

Group with Confidence
(continued)

Unexpected elements create especially interesting vignettes, as this kitchen (below) proves. Warmed by the whimsy of old soldiers apparently poised for battle, the area also gets its snug appeal from a wood stove set before a wonderfully worn fireplace surround. The mantel's peeling paint and the patina of a large copper container (originally an insert in an old washing machine) lend more nostalgia and antiquity to the sunny spot.

Even a minuscule bit of floor space can showcase a beloved treasure or two *(top left)*. Here, pitchers crowd cozily atop an old shaving table, set before a narrow window and framed by plain curtains. The pieces are a mix of Guatemalan majolica and the artist-owner's own kindred creations.

Similarly, it only takes a few well-chosen collectibles to flavor a room *(bottom left)* with sentiment. In this suburban bedroom, a prized sleigh bed is softened by Austrian lace curtains and hand-embroidered linen pillowcases. A 19th-century tin sconce, floral band boxes, and a framed baby picture suggest simple pleasures and simpler times.

137

The Collector's Art
One Fine Thing

Experienced collectors live by a simple rule: Buy the best you can afford, even if it means that your collection grows slowly. Fortunately, it takes only one fine item—a stunning collectible or a beautifully crafted piece of furniture—to turn a simply good room into an unforgettable one. With the help of an oversized accent, even novice antiquers can build character in a home.

Once valued primarily for their storage space, decades-old cupboards, cabinets, hutches, and armoires like this one (top, right) today are prized equally for the architectural quality they impart to even the smallest of spaces. This antique pine version lends grandeur, both in terms of style and height, to a 12x12-foot attic bedroom.

Folk art pieces like the hobby horse (bottom right) make a commanding focal point. This 1870

horse from New England still is clad in its original horse hair, bridle, and saddle.

*In the room **opposite**, the "one fine thing" is a folk art quilt, hung on the wall for maximum impact. Stitched in the 1800s, the patriotic textile piece has special meaning for its owners. The unusual eagle design, a lucky find, reflects their love of the American symbol.*

Special Additions

Country rooms thrive on change. Simple, honest furnishings mix with ease, adapting—chameleonlike— to their surroundings. From a touch of lace to a piece of painted furniture, these "Special Additions" will help set a memorable mood.

Painted Furniture

Few things lift the spirits of a country room like a piece of painted furniture. Homey in hue and engaging in design, even a single painted treasure can season an entire room with color and character.

The beauty of painted furniture is more than skin deep. Each piece recalls the decorative impulse of a country artisan, for whom paint was an elixir to turn humble cabinetry into something finer. The simplest pieces may wear just a single color of paint—an expedient, but pleasing, cover-up for inferior woods. More intricate examples are grain-painted to simulate fine wood, or bear imaginative folk art motifs.

Simple or fancy, painted furniture is among today's most prized collectibles and, as the next pages show, a beautiful addition to any country decor.

A jubilee of country color, the living room (left) mixes painted furniture with vibrant folk art. Among the prized pieces are an 1820s cupboard, still lively in red and green, and a rare turtle decoy, set atop a blanket box.

Painted Furniture
A Colorful Legacy

Country artisans left behind an array of painted styles, from plain-painted primitives to exquisite imitations of aristocratic fashion. Though rarely in pristine condition, painted pieces wear their age gracefully: Faded colors and worn-bare patches simply heighten the sense of history.

Crackled with age, the paint on the 1840s jelly cupboard (left) has proved its staying power. Unlike many primitive pieces, it escaped later stripping or repainting.

Grain paint and cutouts embellish the stool (below) in a blend of folksy and formal styling. The painter combed and puttied mustard-brown paint over pine to create an exaggerated grain.

Imaginatively painted furnishings, such as the document box (above), are highly sought after. This box, made around 1800, bears a fanciful fern-leaf design.

Worn but proud, the Pennsylvania Dutch cupboard (opposite) seems to glow from within. Splendid pieces like this deserve center stage and simple surroundings.

Finely crafted and painted with classical motifs, the circa-1830 chair (above) is a country version of Greek Revival styling. Gold paint mimics costly gilt.

144

Painted Furniture
Country Romance

With fluid lines and fanciful decoration, some painted country pieces can be surprisingly genteel. Country romantics particularly prize "cottage" furniture, like the bed at *left*, decorative, factory-produced, painted pieces of the late 1800s. Although the machine age curtailed the art of furniture painting, today's artisans are reviving it with beautiful results.

*Though different in style, each of these country pieces generates a strong emotional appeal. Painted by Marie Colette, the chest (**above**) celebrates the evocative folk style of Alsace, France—a cousin of Pennsylvania-German design.*

*A 200-year-old Scandinavian chair (**left**) bears a simpler motif, newly painted by Swedish craftsmen.*

Right: *Elegant neoclassical lines grace a country sofa made in Ontario about 1860.*

Painted Furniture
Update On Classics

*This splayed-leg end table, **left**, sports a coat of antique green. Green, along with mustard, brown, yellow, red, and milk-paint blue, were favorite colors for early painted furniture.*

The irresistible appeal of paint on wood has spawned zesty, modern versions of country favorites. Here's a sampling.

*The yellow-painted settee, **above**, is adapted from a bench that once sat in a Pennsylvania cooperage shop. Simple but graceful, the design shows Shaker influence. The drawers below stored tools.*

*Country-simple on the outside, the armoire, **above**, features adjustable shelves for convenient storage.*

*The stenciled chair, **left**, reproduces Lambert Hitchcock's famous design, first manufactured in the early 1800s.*

*Like the originals, today's painted pieces can spice up a room full of antiques or instantly countrify a contemporary setting. Although many feature authentic colors, others, **opposite**, go for the bold.*

Linens And Lace

White linens and lace celebrate the romantic side of life. Crisp, cool, and timeless, the very fiber of these textiles is interwoven with fond memories: fresh-starched sheets on a childhood bed, tiny stitches on a christening gown, an heirloom cloth for holiday tables.

It's no wonder, then, that these nostalgic fabrics, fancy though they may be, are perfectly at ease in country surroundings. Indeed, mixed with mellow woods and country patterns, fine whitework can take on surprisingly homey airs.

Even in rustic settings, though, the romance is undeniable: For those who are sentimental at heart, a touch of linens and lace will help create rooms to linger in.

Linen-dressed sofas, piled with lacy pillows, promise sink-down comfort in this romantic room. Antique pine, dried flowers, and natural textures keep things in a country mood.

151

Linens and Lace
The Heirloom Look

S ince Colonial times, fine linens and lace have been cherished heirlooms, handed down from one generation to the next. Though not everyone is lucky enough to have antique linens tucked away in a drawer, contemporary alternatives allow anyone to savor their luxury.

*Many of today's lace panels and valances **(left)** come in easy-care fabrics, with eyes that simply thread on a curtain rod. Designs include florals, country motifs such as geese, and intricate overall patterns.*

***Opposite:** Old-time elegance and country ease blend in this lace-touched dining room. In a countrified window treatment, shiny chintz and French lace show no trace of fussiness.*

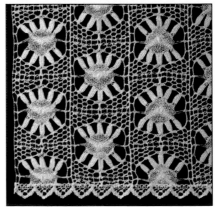

*Heavy lace adorns a linen blanket cover **(above)**. It also can be used to* dress a table, hang as drapes, or provide yardage for slipcovers.

*Wispy crochet patterns **(above)**, Victorian in flavor, look like they once* hung in Grandma's front parlor.

A Touch Of Romance

The bedroom is a natural place to indulge a penchant for linens-and-lace decorating. Serene and sentimental, white finery brings home country-inn romance every day.

Crisp, trimmed sheets offer a fresh-faced counterpoint to the pattern of vintage country quilts and homespun textiles, *right.* Or, blended into an all-white medley, *above,* they create a subtle interplay of shadow, texture, and creamy color.

Today's bed linens make it easy to dress up, with bedding collections lavishly bordered in eyelet or lace. Many are lovely enough to sew into curtains and other fabric treatments.

The two faces of lace: dressy ***(above),*** *for an 18th-century tester bed, or country casual* ***(right).***

In this casual setting, lacy accents—eyelet-edged sheets, a tablecloth, the window panel—tie together old quilts and a mix of patterns. The window panel is a simple table runner, pinned beneath a poufed shade.

Linens and Lace
Soft, Sunny Windows

A touch of lace at the window has a near-magical power to soften a room, relieving austere angles, filtering the sun's rays, and letting in gentle glimpses of the countryside beyond. These inviting window treatments prove the point.

Relaxed and romantic, a lacy square tablecloth (right) comes out of the drawer and onto the window. Fold it in half, separating the corners slightly, then tuck the folded edge over the rod.

***Opposite:** Lace takes to unexpected settings. Here, a floral design mixes beautifully with more traditional shutters and swag.*

***Above:** A contrasting valance works well with cafe curtains, especially when the lace is cottage casual. For a finishing touch, shirr the same material over the curtain rod. Or, use grosgrain ribbon to cover the rod.*

***Above:** Sometimes, simple is best. These voile panels just loop over the curtain rod for a country-elegant look. You can adjust the lacy points so the curtain hangs longer or shorter.*

Special Additions
Country Rugs

Like many decorative treasures from our rural past, country rugs combine folkish artistry with down-home practicality. A testimony to thrift, these colorful accents often were crafted from scraps of leftover fabric.

Woven, hooked or braided, country rugs display a a richness of texture and pattern that warms the heart, as well as the floor. Old, handcrafted rugs are highly collectible and still can be found at auctions, at antique shows and shops, and through specialty rug dealers.

The popularity of antique rugs has prompted a new generation of country-style floor coverings. For a fresh twist on old favorites, investigate the work of modern-day artisans, who are creating one-of-a-kind works adapted from traditional methods. Especially affordable, manufactured designs—including colorfully woven rag rugs—put the charm of the past within easy reach of almost everyone.

As country rugs have risen in stature and price, they also have moved upward in decorative placement. Hung gallery-style on plain painted walls (right), these handmade antiques have all the impact of modern canvases. The pieces—a mix of Amish hooked rugs, Shaker rugs, folk art designs, and a braided classic—join with kindred quilts, folk art, and a reproduction Shaker table. Underfoot, simple woven runners overlap to cozy up the dining spot, lending a bit of antiquity to the carpeted floor.

Country Rugs

American Favorites

Contemporary adaptations of country classics bring the textures and designs of the past into the present. More than mere copies of time-honored rugs, the pieces shown here use fresh colors, materials, or techniques to keep alive the spirit of ingenuity.

More than anything else, homespun textures give country rugs their appeal, as shown by these handcrafted examples (right).

An Amish "dust catcher" (top) is the most richly textured of all country rugs. Originally made by sewing strips of worn clothing to a backing, the design has been adapted here with dyed leather strips.

Center: Simple and elegant, this "floor coverlet" by artisan Sheree White Sorrells is a vintage textile pattern that has been worked into a rug-weight floor accent.

Bottom: Spirited colors and fat braids give new life to a hand-braided oval.

Traditional in design, nubby rag rugs (left) weave sprightly color and pattern into a living room.

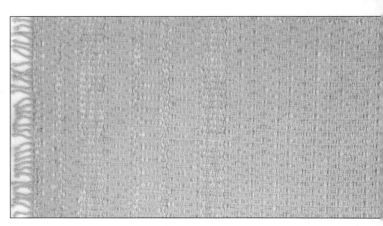

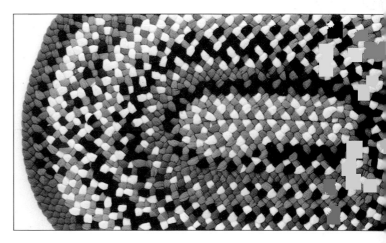

Lighthearted Pastels

Soft and casual, countrified pastel rugs can quickly turn a cold-weather retreat into a springtime haven—or create sunny ambience all year long. Worked in fresh colors, these classic floor treatments are pretty, easy to clean, and suitable for use over wood or carpet.

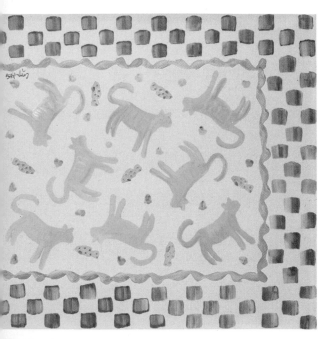

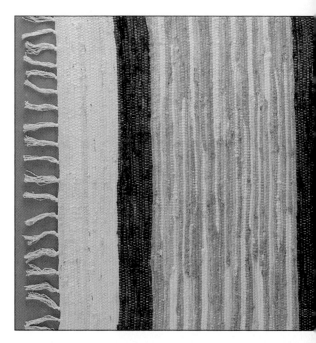

*Today's painted floorcloths can be formal or fanciful. In a witty version **(top left)** by artist Kathy Cooper, yellow tabbies frolic within a checkerboard of pink and white.*

*Affordably priced, cotton rag rugs and runners **(top right)** let you indulge in quick-change decorating artistry.*

***Bottom left:** Casual crocheted rugs are perfect for pastels. They can be custom-crafted from your own fabric.*

*Made of polished chintz, Johanna Erickson's hand-woven rug **(bottom right)** offers deep color and a special glow.*

***Far right:** In a room setting, soothing colors and touch-me textures exude comfort. Weaver Sara Hotchkiss works rich pastels into her thick, diamond-patterned rug.*

Country Rugs
Romantic Rugs

An heirloom-quality investment, this needlepoint rug is a masterpiece of design. The variety of scale, from the finely detailed border to the large central medallion, enriches the piece.

Romance is definitely afoot these days. From needlepoint carpets to hand-painted designs, blooming rugs strew petals at your feet, providing garden-fresh color anywhere. These rugs are only a sample of the dozens of floral "bouquets" available today.

This chintz-inspired design **(right)**, painted by artists Jennifer Day and Ellie Ernst, turns a sisal mat into a colorful room accent that can fit both formal and casual settings.

A gardenlike rug **(opposite)** romances this country English setting. The sitting spot mixes mellow pine with the relaxed rug design for a casual ambience.

This charming hooked rug was crafted in the 1930s or '40s—a time when, as now, a country-cottage revival was leading homeowners down the garden path to romance.

Bordered by lush roses and ribbons, this colorful reproduction of an antique carpet **(left)** says "country" with an English accent. The rug, a replica of a piece woven in Wilton, England, in the 1840s, suggests the grace of a vintage manor house and, thus, works beautifully with refined, rather than rustic, country furnishings.

Special Additions

Change-of-Mood Seating

Part of the enduring appeal of country style is the ease with which elements mix, match, and change with a mood or the seasons. Through crafts and stitchery, even basic seating pieces can take on a fresh new look when it's time for a decorative change of pace.

In these rooms, for example, wicker chairs and a pine table or two, gathered around the fireplace, provide the makings of a great, down-home hideaway. But with different slipcovers and accessories, the ambience changes from cabin cozy to open and airy.

In the scene, *opposite,* shiny white-painted wicker—usually associated with porches and romance—takes on unexpected warmth thanks to the addition of woolly red-and-black cushions. With a plaid rug and horsey accents, the setting is fit for a fireside.

At the first sign of spring, the same room slips into something more comfortable, *below,* with slipcovers made of crisp ticking. For even more lighthearted style, brighten the floor with airy straw matting, the tables with starchy lace, and the mantle with an al fresco scene.

Change-of-Mood Seating
Softly Slipcovered

Slipcovers are a beautiful—and budget-conscious—way to create a decorative change of scene or unify a room. These softly skirted examples make it easy to camouflage a bentwood, countrify a wing chair, or fit modern-day director's chairs into an English country setting.

Turn an austere bentwood into a Victorian-style accent (above). With its shirred skirt and waist-high bows, this great cover-up creates a frilly pinafore effect.

Sewn from a Better Homes and Gardens Designs for Butterick pattern, padded slipcovers (right) make director's chairs elegant enough for tea.

Instead of fussy florals, skirted white slipcovers (left) lighten this log-cabin setting. With their well-used look, the easy-care slipcovers set the old-lodge mood that the owners wanted.

Change-of-Mood Seating
Country Crafted

Some of the most captivating country touches are those that are crafted by hand. Just a bit of stitchery can change chairs and sofas into truly personal, one-of-a-kind accents. The ideas here combine handiwork and Yankee ingenuity, with beautiful results.

Try this idea to create the coziness of needlepoint chair pads without all the work. Instead of filling an entire seat cover, needlepoint the centers of the seats (left), then sew on a patchwork surround. Barn-red paint pulls it all together.

*If you can weave a pot holder, you can create the wonderfully nubby chair seat, **left.***

Weave it from sewn-together strips of sturdy fabrics. To set up the warp strips, securely staple a strip to the seat's right dowel; wrap up and around the right dowel, and down and around the left. Over-and-under strips weave from back to front; pull them straight back under the chair to begin the next row.

Rag rugs cover more than floors today. Pairing the rustic with the refined, this homeowner accented a log sofa with hardy rag-rug cushions (right), then surprised the setting with curlicued wicker and a mix of needlepoint and floral pillows.

Country Interiors

Country interiors express enduring values: simple comforts, a respect for heritage, a drawing close of family and friends. Romantic or rustic, sentimental or spare, country rooms bring us home to the good things in life.

Abloom With Change

Gretchen and Mowry Mann are incurable revisionists, for whom part of the fun of owning a house is constantly remaking it. Their Connecticut home, says Gretchen, "will probably keep evolving until it gets to the point that it is just saturated. We have an irresistible urge to find and change."

When the couple bought the 1920s dwelling two years ago, Gretchen painted the living room white and filled it with dark-stained antiques, chintz sofas, and the gilded trappings of the English country look. Just months later, she decided to simplify, trading in formal finery for scrubbed pine and homey accents, *left.*

In search of a fresh look, Gretchen surrounded her garden-print sofas with scrubbed pine, linen curtains, and white ironstone (left.)

An inveterate and inventive mixer, Gretchen relishes the unexpected. Thus, 18th-century French grave-markers stand tall on either end of the dish-filled cupboard, and dried hydrangeas (above) soften a stern portrait.

175

Folk Art Character

Outside, Lisa and Mark McCormick's Illinois farmhouse is an unassuming frame cottage. Inside, it's a virtual folk art gallery, alive with the character of pieces made by common hands. Spare surroundings play up the color, shapes, and craftsmanship of each piece.

By stripping the living and dining rooms down to their architectural essentials, Mark and Lisa McCormick spotlight the handmade antiques that they love. Silhouetted against the plain walls and bare windows, a vintage whirligig commands attention in the corner. Nearby, a table from the mid-1800s displays a finely detailed Victorian birdhouse. To its right, a pedestal elevates a larger birdhouse to high art.

In the adjacent dining room *(above)*, the same pared-down approach singles out a hand-hooked rug, an old grain bin, and tin fans used over the doorway. In this context, even the antique-framed "doodle" to the left of the doorway—Lisa's masterpiece from the sixth grade—assumes fine-art status.

Log Cabin Lodgings

Located in Minnesota, this modern-day log house sits snugly among trees next to a quiet, sun-sparkled lake. Designed for year-round living, the dwelling is rustic, but not over-poweringly so. In the family room, log walls abut brick, creating visual interest and avoiding the monotony of a single building material.

All of the furnishings were chosen with comfort in mind, as was their fireplace-oriented arrangement. Fabrics are a balance between rustic and refined: The sofa is upholstered in a sportive hunting lodge plaid, and the wing chairs are elegantly slip-covered in country-house white.

Though it boasts a deer head over the mantel (right) and moose antlers on one wall (above), this lakeside log house is not overloaded with woodsy whatnots and backcountry clichés. Furnishings are a mix of casual, contemporary, and family pieces, and the area rug is antique Oriental. On the mantel, a fine collection of "flow-blue" platters echoes the blue hues of the rug.

Country Living Rooms
New England Ensemble

You needn't live in a vintage dwelling to capture the look of earlier times. This house dates from the 1950s, but the ambience is pure old New England. Stenciled walls and hardwood floors provide a period backdrop for the furnishings: a combination of early American antiques and new reproductions. Accessories, slowly accumulated over a period of years, add greatly to the room's old-fashioned feeling.

To make the living room (above) look more spacious, the owners eliminated a standard sofa and created a comfortable window seat instead. Flanked by two chairs, and fronted by an antique painted chest, the window seat "sofa" is a practical—and pretty—solution for the small room.

Facing the main seating area is the "lawyer wall" (opposite), so called because it's dominated by paintings of lawyers; the small, round one dates from the 19th century. Two chairs, both reproductions, bracket the setting and direct attention toward artwork. The grain-painted store chest is a 19th-century piece from Vermont.

Country Living Rooms
A Lively Colonial

Tempered by a light touch, even traditional furnishings can take on fresh airs. The owners of the family room at *right* have filled their home with Colonial antiques, yet avoided creating rooms that look stuck in another century. The family room was given a new country focus by covering formal seating pieces in colorful, free-spirited fabrics—and by letting the simplicity of 18th-century pieces shine through.

From floor to ceiling, this family room is filled with surprises. A candy-stripe cotton fabric dresses the windows and covers the camelback sofas, keeping them from looking straitlaced; a colorful Persian carpet puts geometry on the floor. Putty-colored woodwork and ceiling beams offer a sophisticated alternative to rustic wood.

The family's antiques include a green-painted corner cupboard and circa-1780 bow-back Windsor chairs.

Country Dining Rooms
Romantic Settings

Dining at Susan Davidson's home is an experience to nourish the spirit, as well as the body. A lover of art, Americana, and fine cuisine, Susan serves up satisfying portions of each in her 1857 Missouri cottage.

In the dining room, *opposite,* a tantalizing mix of soft fabrics, old quilts, and painted furniture surrounds diners with richness. At the center is an elegantly simple pine harvest table, its base still showing the original pumpkin paint. The graceful curves of step-back Windsor chairs add a touch of softness.

Susan's cottage-size dining room **(opposite)** *holds a wealth of treasures, including choice quilts displayed on a blanket rack. Fine antiques flank the window: on one side, a 150-year-old blanket chest; on the other, a walnut pie safe made in Ohio circa 1850.*

Heirlooms set a romantic table for guests **(below).** *The china, set atop French place mats, was hand-painted by Susan's great-aunt; goblets are early American glass from New England. Pretty in pinks and greens, the setting echoes colors of the Amish quilt draped nearby.*

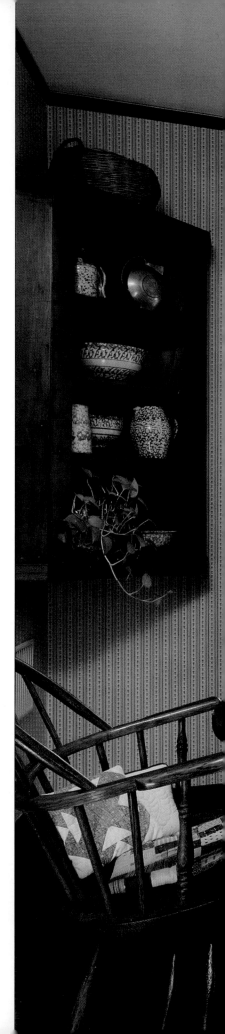

Country Classics

Without doubt, the Windsor is the chair of choice in a great many country-style decorating schmes. And no wonder. The Windsor is a true classic: timeless in design, enduring in appeal, and comfortably at home in plain and fancy surroundings. The dining areas, *above* and *right,* demonstrate the versatility of these shapely American staples.

These days, it's a lucky collector who comes across a matched set of antique Windsor chairs. But here **(opposite)** it happened. The owner found—and snapped up—a set of six chestnut arm chairs, four of which are pictured. Topped with patchwork cushions, the chairs befit the homey attitude of this breakfast nook.

Stripped of cushions and placed in a formal milieu, Windsor chairs look stately. These armless bow-backs **(above)** are perfectly scaled for the small (11½-foot-square) room.

In Keeping With Tradition

I t's hard to believe that the keeping room at *left* isn't nearly as old as the 1806 house in which it is located. When the present owners bought the house, nearly every room had been beautifully—and authentically—restored. But not this one. Though it was billed as a keeping room/kitchen, the space lacked architectural detail, and the fireplace—a contemporary raised hearth model—was totally out of character for the Federal-style house. To right the wrongs, a carpenter was retained. Using nothing but top-quality pine paneling, stock moldings, and paint, he created a fireplace wall that is handsomely true to tradition.

After giving the keeping room its architectural due, the owners turned their attention to furnishings. Most unusual is the dining table, a lovely piece made from an antique quilting frame and old floorboards. The graceful chairs are old, as is the circular double-hooked rug.

189

Light and Inviting

I t's one thing to dream of finding the "perfect" country house and another to actually do so. More often than not (unless money is no object), it's necessary to settle for a would-be perfect house: a sleeping beauty in need of love, hard labor, and numerous repairs.

But along with the backaches and blisters comes the freedom to create countrified living spaces—like the dining rooms here—that are sweetened by contemporary volume and light.

The informal dining area (above) is but one of many renovated rooms in a 1730s New England house. Rather than restore it to its original appearance, the owners opted to update it, combining old and new. The matte white ceramic floor tiles fall into the latter category; the hutch, counters, and English stools are antique.

The delightful dining room opposite is located in a once-dilapidated Napa Valley farmhouse— a house that the real estate agent referred to as "a dog." It took a Cinderella treatment to transform the room. New French doors banish darkness and gloom, and a bath of white paint enhances the airy brightness.

Country Porches
A Place in The Sun

Enclosed or unbounded, porches just naturally breathe country airs. With their broad expanses of glass, screen, and open space, porches invite the outdoors in, creating a tantalizing mix of nature and shelter, of architecture and environment.

The glassed-in Texas porch at *left* proves the power of sunlight. Rough-hewn wood beams, primitive walls, and a flagstone floor seem almost delicate when softened by the sun and surrounded by greenery.

The porch itself is a hybrid of early Texas architectural styles. Originally part of an 1840s cabin, the porch was enclosed when the cabin was adjoined to another home of the same era. To blend with the main structure, the porch sidewalls were enclosed with *fachwerk,* a German-style construction consisting of a framework of timbers and stone, covered with plaster.

*Once an open front porch, the airy sunroom **(left)** now features walls of windows to let in light. Part of a historic Texas home, the room is furnished with Lone Star antiques, including a daybed with the curved-arm style favored by French settlers.*

Cool, White, And Wicker

Like a hanging swing or a pitcher of lemonade, wicker furniture is part and parcel of the country porch mystique, alive with the sensations of cool breezes, slow conversation, and stretched-out afternoons. Lacy and pristine, white-painted wicker civilizes rustic places and dresses up refined ones.

The screened-in porch **(opposite)** belongs to a tireless doer, a business owner who gardens with a passion, travels throughout the country by car, and indulges in reading, writing, and needlework. But when it's time for a rest, she retreats to the back porch and the peace of white wicker. The freshest blooms from her garden keep her company. Set for high tea, the genteel wicker **(below)** pours out nostalgia along with refreshment. The grouping includes a 1920s oak-and-reed buffet and a rare, French birdcage. Although owner Barbara Ash enjoys dressing her wicker for company, when the lace comes off and the tea set is put away, the mood of the solarium reverts to one of casual relaxation.

A Sea-Lover's Sun Porch

To create an ocean air, Mary Anne painted the pine paneling salty white and sponge-painted the floor to mimic a seashell's pink interior. The seating pieces—all consignment shop finds—are arranged as they might be at a restful seaside cottage. A vignette (above) featuring shells collected from childhood and a small painted seascape substitute for an ocean view.

A country porch is a place of sun and solitude, where daydreams can be indulged and favorite moments remembered. Although Mary Anne Thomson has lived in the Midwest for nearly 20 years, she still longs for the seashore and the ocean-side home where she was raised. But rather than bemoan her landlocked status, she decided to improvise decoratively. On her enclosed sun porch, *left* and *above*, soft colors and childhood keepsakes bring back memories of the sea.

197

Under-the-Rafters Retreat

Bonnie Brown doesn't play favorites. She's as fond of small trinkets as she is of fine treasures, and she's equally admiring of English, French, and American design influences. Her under-the-eaves guest room, *opposite*, reflects her open-minded philosophy—beautifully and harmoniously.

Overnight guests are invariably charmed when introduced to their cozy raftered retreat. Designed to call to mind an auberge in France, the room is furnished with a mix of homey American heirlooms, French fabrics, and English artwork and accessories. An American hooked rug serves as the snuggery's colorful centerpiece and ties the assemblage together.

199

Country Bedrooms
Four-Poster Character

There's something about a four-poster that makes a person feel grand, and a room *look* grand. It's ideally suited to country settings, and it can always be counted on to infuse a room—be it large or small—with stature.

It looks like a regal antique, but this handsome four-poster (opposite) is a new reproduction. It is the undisputed focal point in this English country bedroom, just as the owner wanted.

Befitting its stately personality is the elegant white lace blanket cover paired with luxuriant down-filled pillows. The background color scheme—soft pink walls and white paneling—is

a perfect accompaniment for this English gentlewoman's theme.

Small rooms, too, are accepting of four-posters, as long as they're not too imposing or over-

scaled. This one (below) is Shaker-like in its straightforward simplicity and is a perfect fit—size-wise and style-wise—in this homespun Colonial setting.

Added Pleasures

Luxury is a welcome asset, even in the simplest of country settings. The idea is to indulge—not with showiness or ostentation—but with things that will add to your comfort, pleasure, and personal ease.

This bedroom, *right,* though certainly not opulent, is luxurious nonetheless. The pristine, all-white room is embellished with assorted nonessential extras that serve no other purpose than to please.

Designed to pamper both body and soul, this summer-house bedroom is a place of respite. The star attraction—a Victorian wicker bed—is topped with the plumpest of down pillows and the finest of lacy white sheets. Just a few steps from the bed (above) is an en suite primping area, complete with a built-in wash basin and a well-endowed dressing table.

Sentimental Setting

When Jenny Dolan comes home from college, her room is at the ready. Awaiting her, like faithful friends, are the furnishings, mementos, and special treasures that saw her through her high school days. But the room is by no means little girlish. The new mini-print wallcovering and floral fabrics are reflections of Jenny's maturing tastes. It's just the sentimental associations that have welcomely stayed the same.

A glance around Jenny's room offers quick clues to her twin passions— horses and riding. Her English velvet riding hat sits atop an appropriately named Jenny Lind spool table (above), and an assemblage of hunt scenes, English and American, adorn the wall. Hanging at the foot of her cherry Empire rope bed (opposite) is an antique English hunting horn. Next to the bed, a Hepplewhite-style table holds more equine mementos, a whimsical stuffed cat, and photos of family and friends.

Country Bedrooms
Quilted Comforts

I t's easy to understand why handmade quilts are so prized by fans of country decorating. Not only can they be counted on to add instant color and pattern to a room, many offer—via stitchery—interesting glimpses into America's past. Many of our earliest quilts were made by young girls for their hope chests, and often, their intricate patterns depict images, events, and occurrences of the times. But whether they tell a story or not, quilts are highly individualized expressions of needlework artistry, and are guaranteed to benefit any kind of country setting.

It took nothing more than the addition of a star-studded quilt to turn this bedroom **(opposite)** into a masterpiece. Fortuitously, the blue-green of the quilt mimics the painted hues of the mantel, an old beauty that the owner found in Ohio.

A pair of red and white quilts, both dating from the late 1800s, add zing to this twin-bedded room **(above)**. The same red is repeated on the walls, where stenciled strawberries colorfully wend their way around the room.

Tucked-Away Quarters

P art of the charm of old country houses are the nooks and crannies—odd snippets of space, passed along through the years to challenge the imagination and ingenuity of each successive owner. The bedrooms, *right* and *above,* both occupy tiny, tucked-away spaces in old homes that were recently renovated. Wisely, the owners left the quirky spaces intact for yet another generation to enjoy their special character.

Though just a sliver of space, the room (above) is filled with boyish character, from its folk art animals to sailboats perched on a ledge. The young occupant was treated by his father to a charming stenciled floor, the motifis based on a design seen on a Williamsburg blanket chest.

The low-slung lines of a farmhouse attic (right) get a decorative lift from color, old and new. The sugar loaf quilt dates from 1890; the contemporary painting is by the owner. A newly added skylight helps relieve the low ceiling line.

Kitchens
And Baths

By nature, kitchens and baths are hardworking spaces, the domains of modern-day efficiency. Country, with its soothing balm of texture and heritage, transforms them from places where we *have* to be, to places where we *want* to be.

A Sunny Mix of Old and New

A variety of ingredients makes this newly built kitchen, and adjacent keeping room, a treat for the country connoisseur. With creative sleight of hand, the owners have melded modern amenities with old-time adornments, forging a kitchen that's as charming as it is convenient.

The clever use of salvaged building materials belies the room's recent vintage. The yellow pine countertops once did duty in an old hotel, and the ceiling beams hail from an 1820s stagecoach stop.

*It took the owners two years to decide on a color for the cabinets, but the final choice, a vibrant green, was worth the wait. Windows (**right**) trimmed in red, add spice to the scheme, as do lace valances, geraniums, and a ledge adorned with collectibles. The color scheme carries into the keeping room (**above**).*

A Sunny Mix
Of Old and New
(continued)

Boasting lovely mullioned windows, a floor made from 1x10-inch aged pine shelving, and a fireplace fashioned from an 1850s stone wall, this keeping room is a haven of welcome and warmth. Skylights shed extra light on the modern-day colonial scheme.

*True to colonial tradition, the fireplace **(above)** is the heart of this keeping room, and is in full view of the kitchen, the delightful dining area **(left)**, and even the bake center **(right)**. Simple farmhouse furnishings, including a rustic pine table, an old pie safe, and a pair of adirondack rocking chairs, are naturals in this homey setting.*

Country French, Country Fresh

The owners of this kitchen took a cosmetic approach to creating country French flavor, *right*, in an existing kitchen and breakfast nook. Wood-grain cabinets were left intact, but given Gaelic oomph with crisp white paint banded in blue. Portuguese tiles in a French motif invest the new center island and sink area with color, pattern, and provincial élan. Other au courant elements include teak flooring and a wall covered in polished paving bricks.

Blue and yellow are classic color choices for a country French scheme. Here the colors flow from the kitchen proper (above) to an informal dining area (right). The nook is beguilingly furnished with antique rush-seat chairs, a skirted table, and très French tiebacks.

Kitchens and Baths
Colored by Collections

The owner of this kitchen can't say no—at least to Americana. One of her greatest pleasures is collecting, and her kitchen, like every room in her home, is bedecked with her finds. The assemblage isn't just for display: Many of the wares are used regularly.

An aura of yesteryear pervades the breakfast nook (opposite), with its small rustic table, country cupboard, and two New York State ladderback chairs. Stenciled walls—done by the homeowner—and wedgwood blue paint trim embellish the colonial scheme.

Amidst baskets, dried herbs, and collections of stoneware, wooden bowls, colorful firkins, rolling pins, gameboards, and assorted jugs, the kitchen (above) has all the conveniences a country-loving cook could want.

Home for a Country Cook

The most pleasing country kitchens are those that reflect the owners' interests. This one, in a renovated 1750s New England farmhouse, does just that. The homeowner is a dedicated gardener, who also delights in preserving and preparing what she grows. Bounties from the garden—culinary herbs, fresh vegetables, and home-canned preserves—are stored and displayed in the open, with decorative (and mouth-watering) results.

Year-round, this kitchen is bathed in light and filled with summery scents. Dried herbs hang from centuries-old ceiling beams (above), and fresh plants thrive on the ledge of a newly added bay window (opposite).

Farmhouse Contemporary

Placed within easy earshot of the sleek kitchen work area (opposite) is a new version of an old trestle table and four antique English ladder-back chairs. Here, friends and family members can visit with Fran as she cooks.

Fran Lechtrecker made a wise move when she decided to turn four tiny rooms in her 1890s house into a single spacious, and gracious, eat-in kitchen. With its sleek cabinetry and warm, farmhouse-style table, the new space combines the best of contemporary and country influences. The result is a room geared not just to cooking, but to dining, entertaining, and relaxing good times as well.

Diners who face the French doors (above) are treated to a view of a lovely garden. A scrubbed-pine chest displays Fran's collection of blue-and-white china.

223

Kitchens and Baths
European Simplicity

In the main cooking area (opposite), wood cabinets—stacked to the ceiling farmhouse-style—and floors add warmth. Granite-look countertops and a pink-painted ceiling provide unexpected panache.

Once a separate screened-in porch, the sunroom (above) is now part of the restyled, eat-in, live-in kitchen. Furnished with wicker, an antique English washstand, and a boldly colorful rug, the glass-walled room invites all comers to sit back and bask in the sun.

In this newly remodeled kitchen, country expresses itself in a subtle whisper, not a commanding shout. In styling the space, the owners, an architect and his wife, chose not to limit themselves to a single decorative look. Instead, they opted for a "mixed breed"—a classic melding of cherished antiques, European-inspired cabinets, and high-style accents.

As in many remodelings, serendipity flavored the results. The fir-and-poplar cabinets were intended for painting, but proved too beautiful to cover.

Kitchens and Baths

Country Baths: Add Ambience

There are many ways to bring "country" to a bathroom, but few things do the job as thoroughly as antique fixtures and period finishes. Beadboard and wood accents keep the bath, *opposite*, farmhouse simple, while ornate tile work, *below*, recalls Victorian fancies.

Sometimes all it takes is the addition of a fabulous fixture to make a big splash. In this new-house bath **(opposite)**, the scene-setter is a restored antique pedestal wash basin, a beauty that was purchased for its old-world appeal. An antique washstand befits the early-days theme.

Country Victorian best describes the bathroom **(right)**, remodeled as part of a whole-house renovation. The owners, avid antiquers, spent years hunting for the appropriate period fixtures, including the high-tank commode, the pedestal basin, and the fanciful brass wall sconces. The decorative tiles—all 120 pounds of them—were found on a trip to London, and hand-carried home.

Warmed With Color

Warm, sunny colors just naturally say "country." So when these baths needed a pick-me-up, the owners plucked schemes from nature's own palette. The crisp yellow-striped fabric, *right*, was glued to walls with wallpaper paste; the matching sink skirt hooks onto wood strips glued inside the sink, so it's easy to wash. In the room *above*, a rich shade of apricot perks up the tiny space.

*A splash of yellow fabric revitalized the vintage bath, **right**. For added punch, the owner added a display shelf and nubby rug. **Above:** A lively wallpaper and coordinating, apricot-colored curtains play up the warm tones of a pine washstand.*

Dressed Up With Paint

Some of the prettiest country baths start with simple settings. The two baths shown here were strictly plain-vanilla until paint, pastel colors, and nostalgic furnishings transformed them into havens of country charm. Slender bureaus add storage space and character.

Several coats of fresh white paint and an assortment of nothing-fancy finishing touches are what make this old-fashioned bathroom (below) so fetching.

The bureau is a thrift-store find, also treated to a coat of color. A green-painted floor and pastel accents enliven the scheme.

Inspired by a garden of dried wildflowers hanging overhead, the owners of this new bathroom **(below)** painted all of the cabinets and woodwork a soft shade of rose, and covered the walls in a country-check wallpaper. Filled with flowers, the antique wicker doll pram on the counter is a fanciful prop.

Rustic Settings

Rugged stone and glowing woods make this bathroom (left) a standout. The antique maple dry sink (fitted with a basin) warms the setting, as do the tiger maple mirror and the heirloom hand towels. Also atmospheric is the bath (above), with its wide-board cabinets and sink fashioned from an old stone mortar.

For true aficionados of the country look, atmosphere is everything. Great care is taken to create an authentic aura of rusticity, not just in the main living areas of the house, but in less-frequented rooms as well.

Located in a converted barn, the bathroom, *left,* is blessed with atmosphere aplenty. To enhance the natural setting, the owners have furnished it simply with a mellow dry-sink-turned-vanity. In contrast, the bath *above* summons rustic aura with imagination and rough-hewn materials. The cabinets are built of centuries-old flooring.

233

Country Gardens

Gardens let us grow a bit of country all our own. The sweet smell of a rose or the creak of a garden swing transports us to another time and place—and reminds us that life is a continuum of past and present, and a future filled with springtimes.

Country Gardens
Attuned To Nature

The country life-style evokes words like natural, welcoming, and unpretentious. On their one-acre, riverside lot, Andy and Elizabeth Rocchia have captured those same enduring qualities in a garden that brims with comfort and character.

A lesson in good garden design, the pastoral hillside, *above* and *right,* mimics conditions in nature to achieve an unplanned look. The secret to its beauty and longevity is the careful selection of plants that work *with* the environment, not against it. Free-flowing flower beds, separated by winding paths, are filled with unstructured plantings of both wild and cultivated species, combined to offer color from spring to fall. *continued*

Above: One of seven minigardens, the herb patch is an informal mix of thyme, sage, lavender, oregano, fennel, foxglove, and mint. At the center is an ornamental bee skep, made of woven straw and displayed on dry, sunny days.
Right: Flowering bulbs and early-blooming perennials, such as calla lily, poppy, and foxglove, predominate in the spring garden. A nylon wind kite flutters in the tree for portable color.

Attuned To Nature

(continued)

Left: Conjuring up memories of lazy summer afternoons, a simple wooden swing serves as a reminder that, after the day's work is finished, the garden should be enjoyed from the quiet solitude of a grove of trees.

Top right: Bark-covered paths criss-cross the Rocchias' garden. This section of the path meanders through the cottage garden, where such carefree flowers as daylily, canterbury-bells, sweet william, red-hot-poker, and valerian bloom.

Bottom right: Amusing touches help camouflage an old toolshed. Painted on the wall, hollyhocks and an elegant English-style "back" for the bench look real from a distance. A topiary bear, pruned from an overgrown pyracantha, stands guard.

The Rocchias have designed their garden in a delightful series of outdoor "rooms" that stairstep down the hillside to the river; each room is home to a collection of plants with similar needs.

For example, near the river, where the soil is generally soggy, they developed a "bog garden," with moisture-loving plants such as Japanese iris and ferns. Farther up the slope, *left* and *top,* where conditions are drier, are the "meadow garden" and the cutting garden, filled with bulbs and woodland flowers that require a well-drained soil. Throughout each of the seven minigardens, colors and textures change from month to month, depending on what's in bloom.

Despite the careful structure, the ambience of the garden is country-casual and very relaxed, like the Rocchias' life-style. The couple delights in adding outdoor art and sculpture, much of it Elizabeth's own work. When nature fails to perform on cue, these outdoor accessories can be moved wherever color and focus are needed.

Country Gardens
City Sanctuary

Above: Layers of color add dimension to this modest yard, where the red and pink hues of tulips, azaleas, and a flowering cherry herald spring.
Left: Peggy believes a city garden calls for special richness. A luxuriant display of old-fashioned roses, daylilies, poppies, campanula, and perennial bachelor's-buttons seems to transplant her cottage to the countryside.

For Peggy Conklin, memories of growing up are laced with images of the countryside: stretched-out land, never-ending views, and pockets of color growing from the earth. Today, by her tiny cottage in Seattle, *left,* Peggy has drawn on those memories to create a little bit of country in the heart of the city.

Bounded by a 40x100-foot lot, Peggy's garden is mindful of urban realities. "The country environment is its own garden," she says. "Here, a garden is a place to go and rest." Accordingly, Peggy has blended texture, color, and structure to create a sanctuary that is private, yet—like the path *above*—fosters an illusion of space.

continued

241

A City Sanctuary

(continued)

Although Peggy's garden has developed through what she calls a "continuous cycle" of change, her vision of an urban oasis has clearly guided each step. Peggy began in the front yard, planting tall flowers and hedges to offer privacy, then added trellises for intimacy at the back. The tiered arches, *opposite,* provide some visual barrier while letting in air and light.

A professional artist, Peggy draws on her innate design sense to arrange the elements within her quiet retreat. "I garden a little bit like a painter in that I build up layers. Rather than having a neat, delineated image, it's more like overlapping texture and richness."

True to her word, Peggy's garden unfolds in subtly blended stages. A rock path outside the cellar door, *lower left,* leads to a tiny patch of lawn, just large enough for a picnic. Beyond the lawn lies the flowering framework of the garden: a stone-strewn planting area filled with iris, delphinium, poppy, and campanula. Old garden roses, which offer prolonged blooming, add backup support to the seasonal bloomers.

Despite her love of spread-out spaces, Peggy finds compensations in constraint. "Being in a smaller garden, one is surrounded by color and richness. It makes something happen that wouldn't have happened in a larger space."

Top left: Diversity in color, foliage type, and flower form make even a narrow border of hostas, peonies, and roses a painterly pleasure.
Bottom left: In Peggy's eye, a pathway is more than the shortest distance between two points. This flagstone path wanders through dense pocket plantings of flowers and foliage, offering closeup views of the colorful clusters of peonies, poppies, and roses.
Opposite: Simple arches offer a permanent backdrop for the fleeting flowers of seasonal perennials, and a visual gateway to Lake Washington. The flowering framework of the spring garden includes iris, delphinium, poppy, and campanula; old garden roses offer more prolonged color.

Country Gardens
Everlasting Gardens

Top right: An everlasting bouquet preserves the bright colors of summer. This basket overflows with xeranthemum, strawflower (helichrysum), statice, and love-in-a-mist seedpods.

Left: A cottage-garden array of favorite cutting flowers is an ideal place to gather blossoms for drying. The blue salvia, in the foreground, dry particularly well.

Bottom right: A drying rack, constructed of wire mesh stapled between a wood frame, lets the air circulate freely for beautiful results.

Fresh flowers may be as fleeting as the summer season, but their beauty can be everlasting. Drying flowers extends the pleasures of a garden into all months of the year.

Almost any flower can be dried, but some species preserve more easily than others. A group of annual flowers, called everlastings, feel papery to the touch even when they're growing. The everlastings—including acroclinium, ammobium, globe amaranth, statice, and strawflower—are grown from seed for flowers the same season.

They mix beautifully in a fresh cutting garden or flower border, then dry to luscious color. For variety, even roadside blossoms and grasses can be dried for everlasting delight. *continued*

245

Everlasting Gardens

(continued)

Perfect dried flowers begin with perfect blooms. Any of the varieties at *right* make excellent candidates for drying.

Air drying is a good method for beginners. Flowers suited for air drying include acroclinium, ammobium, bells-of-Ireland, celosia, globe amaranth, heather, lunaria, salvia, statice, starflower, strawflower, and yarrow.

For best results, flowers should be cut at their peak on a warm, sunny day after the dew evaporates. The leaves are then stripped, and the stems tied in in small bunches with string or elastic ties. The bunches should be hung upside down in a dark, well-ventilated attic or room for two or three weeks.

Silica gel, sold at crafts shops, is a desiccant that quickly absorbs plant moisture. Good candidates for this method of drying include dahlia, delphinium, feverfew, lily, marigold, rose, shasta daisy, and zinnia.

The dessicant method calls for placing a base of 1 to 2 inches of silica gel granules in the bottom of a cookie tin or coffee can. The short-cut stem goes into the drying medium, with the flower faceup and not touching another flower. More granules are sprinkled over the flowers until they are covered to a depth of 1 inch. The tin should be covered tightly and left in a dark, dry place for two to six days. The blooms can be removed when the petals feel papery, then stored in airtight containers. *continued*

Top left: Identified by the raised ridges on its stems, ammobium also is called winged everlasting. The 1- to 2-inch flowers appear in clusters. Cut blooms before they're fully open.
Middle left: Bells-of-Ireland is named for its green bell-shaped calyxes. Cut the whole stalk when flowers are in full bloom.
Bottom: The daisylike pink or white blossoms of helipterum retain their delicate color when dried. Cut the whole stem just before the flower is fully open.

Left: The long, red tassellike flowers of love-lies-bleeding (or amaranth) bring classic beauty to dried bouquets. The name amaranth in Greek means "does not wither."

Above: Strawflowers come in red, purple, yellow, and white. Cut flowers when they're half open; replace stems with florist's tape before you dry the blooms.

Left: Both the colorful cockscomb (or crested) and plumosa (or feathered) types of celosia are extremely long lasting in fresh or dried bouquets. To dry, cut flower heads as soon as they mature, before the black beadlike seeds appear.

Right: The mounding plants of globe amaranth are covered nonstop all summer long with ¾-inch cloverlike blossoms, available in red, pink, yellow, purple, and white. For drying purposes, pick flowers just as they're fully opened.

Everlasting
Gardens

(continued)

To increase the lifespan of dried flowers, never place the stems in water. For structured arrangements, stems are usually anchored in florist's foam; floral wire and tape can lengthen cut-short stems if needed. Damage from dry or humid household air can be prevented by spraying the bouquet with hair spray or clear acrylic; arrangements should be kept away from direct sunlight to avoid fading.

To mix fresh and dried flowers in an arrangement, the stems of dried flowers should be several inches shorter than the stems of the fresh flowers. Then, add just enough water to keep the fresh flowers alive.

Amassed in a smokehouse, *right,* a harvest of everlastings bespeaks the color and glory these blossoms bring to a home. Woven into wreaths, arranged in baskets or crocks, or hung in stark simplicity, *above,* everlastings are as much a part of country settings as warm woods and natural texture.

The one-time smokehouse at **right** *provides the ideal conditions for air drying a gardenful of blooms, but a dark, dry attic or closet will suffice.*

To create an everlasting wreath **(bottom, left)** *wire dried herbs and flowers to an undecorated wreath form made from straw or grapevines.*

Window Box Gardens

It doesn't take a country acreage to enjoy nature's finest splendor. Open the window to your imagination, and even a sill can set the stage for a sunny miniature meadow or shady pocket of blooms. All it takes for a flower-framed view of the world is a box filled with potting soil, closely spaced plants, water, and care.

A window box can be anything that holds soil. The old bicycle basket *(above)* brims with shade-loving ivy, browallia, and impatiens. Other plants for shady sills include begonia, caladium, and coleus.

Flower fantasies come to life in a whimsical window creation *(left)*. The colorful potpourri of plants combines some customary, container-grown flowers like pansy, viola, and fibrous begonia, with a couple of unexpected surprises like the towering dahlias and cleome. Curves and cutouts add charmimg, custom-made details.

Herbs add spice to a kitchen window **(above)**. The recipe: chives, parsley, mint, scented geranium, dusty miller, and nierembergia.

Shutters and ivy-covered bricks set the theme for this formal, traditionally trimmed cedar box **(right)**, filled with geraniums, vinca, and dusty miller.

Weathered, rough-sawn white oak creates a rustic, homespun look for a garage window **(right)**. Planted in a simple color scheme of red geraniums and white petunias, the combination of upright and trailing growth habits produces a full, three-dimensional effect. The 28x5x8-inch box is slightly canted in front so blossoms can cascade over the edge. Other plants for sunny sills include sweet alyssum, celosia, dusty miller, lobelia, dwarf marigold, pansy, sanvitalia, and dwarf zinnia.

Acknowledgments

Field Editors

Bernadette Baczynski
Barbara East Cathcart
Eileen Deymier
Estelle Bond Guralnick
Cathy Howard
Bonnie Maharam
Trish Maharam
Carol Nuckols
Ruth L. Reiter
Mary Anne Thomson
Jessie Walker

Photographers

Alan Abramowitz
D. Randolph Foulds
Susan Gilmore
Karlis Grant
Jim Hedrich/Hedrich–Blessing
Bill Hopkins
William N. Hopkins/Hopkins
  Associates
Peter Krumhardt
Scott Little

Photographers *(continued)*

Maris/Semel
Barbara Martin
Nick Merrick/Hedrich-Blessing
Tommy Miyasaki/De Gennaro
Mike Moreland
William Stites
Tim Street-Porter
Perry Struse
Rick Taylor
Al Teufen
Joan Hix Vanderschuit
John Vaughan
Jessie Walker Associates

Sources

(When writing for information about handcrafts, please include a self-addressed stamped envelope)

Pages 100–103
Sally Cammack
Rte. 6, Mill Creek Rd.
Cynthiana, KY 41031

Pages 104–107
Jeff White
1012 Penn St.
Lebanon, PA 17042

Pages 108–111
William Jauquet
P.O. Box 454
Denmark, WI 54208

Pages 112–115
Jackson of Donovan
P.O. Box 242
Wrightsville, GA 31096

Pages 116–118
Monte Lindsley
P.O. Box 551
Fall City, WA 98024

Page 147
Bottom left: Scan Des
660 Miami Cir.
Atlanta, GA 30324
Top: Maria Colette
29 E. Bells Mill Rd.
Chestnut, Hill, PA 19118

Page 148
Top: Hickory Chair Co.
P.O. Box 2147
Hickory, NC 28603
Center right: The Lane Co.
P.O. Box 151
Altavista, VA 24517–0151
Bottom: Hitchcock Chair Co.
P.O. Box 369
New Hartford, CT 06057
Center left: Nichols and Stone
232 Sherman St.
Gardner, MA 01440

Page 149
Habersham Plantation
P.O. Box 1209
Tocca, Ga 30577

Pages 150–157:
Rue de France
78 Thames St.
Newport, RI 02840
Linen & Lace
4 Lafayette
Washington, MO 63090
paper white, ltd.
P.O. Box 956
Fairfax, CA 94930.

Page 159
Top: Amish Country
Collection
P.O. Box 5084
New Castle, PA 16105
Center: Whitewoven Studio
201½ N. Main St.
Waynesville, NC 28786
Bottom: Rugs, Rugs—
Antiques, Antiques
3313 Knox St.
Dallas, TX 75205

Page 162:
Top left: Orchard House
Floorcloths
Rte. 5, Box 214
Kings, NC 27021
Bottom left: Rugs, Rugs—
Antiques, Antiques
3313 Knox St.
Dallas, TX 75205
Bottom right:
Johanna Erickson
48 Chester St.
Watertown, MA 02172
Top right: Import Specialists
82 Wall St.
New York, NY 10005

Page 163
Sweet Nellie
1262 Madison Ave.
New York, NY 10128

Page 164
Top: Ernest Treganowan
306 E. 61st St.
New York, NY 10021
Center: Day & Ernst, Ltd.
Jennifer Day
1481 Spruce Ave.
Tallahassee, FL 32303.
or
Ellie Ernst
RFD 1, Tanager Ct.
West Point, VA 12181
Bottom right: Stark Carpet
Corp.
D&D Building
979 Third Ave.
New York, NY 10022

Page 210
Terra Designs
241 E. Blackwell St.
Dover, NY 07801

Index